P9-CCS-556

APR 1 0 2012

THE

BHAGAVA

ALSO BY GAVIN FLOOD

An Introduction to Hinduism

The Ascetic Self: Subjectivity, Memory, and Tradition

The Tantric Body: The Secret Tradition of Hindu Religion

ALSO BY CHARLES MARTIN

Signs & Wonders

Starting from Sleep: New and Selected Poems

Metamorphoses (translation)

THE
BHAGAVAD GITA

A NEW TRANSLATION

Gavin Flood and Charles Martin

W. W. Norton & Company
NEW YORK — LONDON

3/97>43

Copyright © 2012 by Gavin Flood and Charles Martin
All rights reserved
Printed in the United States of America
First Edition

For information about permission to reproduce
selections from this book,
write to Permissions, W. W. Norton & Company, Inc.,
500 Fifth Avenue, New York, NY 10110

For information about special discounts for bulk purchases,
please contact W. W. Norton Special Sales at
specialsales@wwnorton.com or 800-233-4830

Manufacturing by Courier Westford
Book design by Brooke Koven
Production manager: Anna Oler

Library of Congress Cataloging-in-Publication Data

Bhagavadgita. English.
The Bhagavad Gita : a new translation / Gavin Flood
and Charles Martin. — First edition.
pages cm
Translated from Sanskrit.
Includes bibliographical references.
ISBN 978-0-393-08165-7 (hardcover)
I. Flood, Gavin D., 1954– translator.
II. Martin, Charles, 1942– translator. III. Title.
BL1138.62.E5 2012
294.5'92404521—dc23

2011052336

W. W. Norton & Company, Inc.
500 Fifth Avenue, New York, N.Y. 10110
www.wwnorton.com

W. W. Norton & Company Ltd.
Castle House, 75/76 Wells Street, London W1T 3QT

1 2 3 4 5 6 7 8 9 0

To our teachers

CONTENTS

Ever since its composition, sometime between the second century BC and the third or fourth century AD, the *Gita* has captivated the Hindu imagination, proving an inspiration to some of India's leading politicians and public figures (such as Mahatma Gandhi) and a generating source of art and literature. And yet, because it deals with common human issues—how we should act, how we should perform virtue in the context of who we are in our own lives—Gandhi justifiably regarded it as a universal text. Still, the *Gita* is a dialogue, rather than a work of systematic philosophy, and so the meanings of the text are not self-evident. As a result, the *Gita* has been interpreted in many ways and used in support of a number of different philosophical and political ideas, from pacifism to aggressive nationalism, from philosophical monism to theism.

As we have said, the *Gita* begins with the moral dilemma of Arjuna. But we need now to say more about that dilemma and the narrative context in which it is set. Although the *Gita* is self-contained, its actions and characters are firmly interwoven with those of a much larger poem, one of the largest ever conceived, a Sanskrit epic of nearly one hundred thousand stanzas called the *Mahabharata*. The *Gita* forms a small but important part of this epic (6.23–40). Complex in its narrative and chronology, the *Mahabharata* tells many stories, but a brief description of the relevant part of the epic will help us to understand the stakes involved in the dialogue between Krishna and Arjuna.

TRANSLATORS' INTRODUCTION

The *Bhagavad Gita*, the "Song of the Lord," is a Sanskrit poem composed in seven hundred numbered stanzas, divided into eighteen chapters, in the form of a dialogue between the Lord Krishna, a god whom we first see in his "gentle, human form," and Arjuna, a heroic warrior, who is himself the son of another god by a mortal woman. Their discourse takes place on the eve of a cataclysmic battle, on a field between two armies of warring cousins. Arjuna, realizing that if he fights, he will be forced to kill his friends, relatives, and teachers, casts down his bow and arrow (he is a great archer) and refuses to engage in combat. The *Gita* unfolds as a discussion of Arjuna's moral dilemma, with Krishna as the wise interlocutor explaining to Arjuna that he must overcome his instinctual revulsion and convincing him that he must attend to his duties as a warrior, while Krishna reveals himself as an incarnation of God in human form.

The *Gita* and the *Mahabharata*

The story into which the *Gita* is set is that of a war between two rival factions over succession to the throne of the North Indian kingdom of Bharata. Both parties have arguments that legitimate their claim. Once upon a time, there were two brothers, sons of Vyasa, who is both the author of the *Mahabharata* and a character in it. The elder son, Dhritarashtra, was born blind and could not inherit the throne, and so his younger brother Pandu became king. Pandu had been cursed, so that he would die if he ever slept with a woman. His resourceful first wife Pritha (also known as Kunti) slept in turn with three gods, producing the first three of five sons; his second wife, Madri, slept with twin gods and produced twins. The five children were known collectively as the Pandavas: Yudhishthira, the eldest, Bhima, the strongest, our protagonist Arjuna, and the twins Nakula and Sahadeva. The other faction consisted of their cousins, the hundred sons of Dhritarashtra, known as the Kauravas, or descendants of Kuru. The Kauravas were led by their eldest brother, Duryodhana.

On the death of King Pandu, blind Dhritarashtra succeeded him, which created rivalry between the two sets of cousins. In an attempt to keep the cousins' rivalry from turning into war, Dhritarashtra divided the kingdom; one half to be ruled by Duryodhana, and the other half by Yudhishthira. Yudhishthira instituted a royal consecration, sanctioned by the Vedic scriptures, to establish his authority, which involved

Duryodhana challenging him to a game of dice. Yudhishthira accepted the challenge and gambled away his kingdom, along with his brothers and their shared wife Draupadi, who was publicly humiliated. A second game of dice, however, yielded a somewhat better outcome, ensuring that he and his brothers, along with Draupadi, would go into exile in the forest for twelve years with a further year spent incognito. Once this period of time had elapsed, the Pandavas could return to reclaim their kingdom.

The *Mahabharata* recounts their time in the forest, the adventures they experienced, and the various religious teachings they encountered. After thirteen years in exile they returned to reclaim their kingdom as agreed, but Duryodhana refused to give it up, and so war ensued. The battle at Kurukshetre (an actual place north of Delhi) lasted for eighteen days, until the Kauravas were utterly defeated by the Pandavas. Set on the eve of this great conflict, in a timeless moment before the storm, the *Bhagavad Gita* itself is removed from the battle, framed by the request of the blind king Dhritarashtra to his minister Sanjaya, behind the Kaurava lines:

> *"Having gathered, battle-hungry*
> *on virtue's field, the field of Kuru,*
> *what did they do then, Sanjaya,*
> *my sons and the sons of Pandu?"*

Sanjaya observes the battle with his divine sight, and recounts the dialogue between Krishna and Arjuna to the king.

Arjuna's charioteer Krishna is a prince of the Vrishni clan

and cousin to both the Pandus and Kauravas. He declared that one side could have his army and the other side could have him in a non-combative role. The Pandavas chose to have Krishna and so he became Arjuna's charioteer while his army was relegated to the Kauravas. Again, Krishna's decision not to side wholeheartedly with one faction reflects the subtlety and complexity of the story; the Kauravas are not straightforwardly the perpetrators of wrong and both sets of cousins have legitimate claims to succession.

The Teachings

The main issues for the *Gita* are therefore issues of ethics and virtue, and the opening lines of the text reflect these fundamental concerns. Dhritarashtra asks Sanjaya to tell him what the Pandavas did "on virtue's field, the field of Kuru" (*dharmakshetre kurukshetre*). The Sanskrit term for virtue is *dharma*, whose semantic range includes duty, law, truth, ethics, and the sociocosmic order. It is from a Sanskrit verbal root *dhri*, meaning "to uphold" or "bear up," and so *dharma* points to a power that upholds the universe and to a natural law that constrains the behavior of all beings. Thus it is the *dharma* of grass to grow, of birds to fly, and of warriors to fight. But it is not only natural law but moral law as well. An ordered society must be virtuous and people must act in accordance with their *dharma*. *Kurukshetre* and the field of virtue represent, of course, the field of life, the field of all our lives. The teachings of the *Gita*, although set within a particular narrative and context, are intended to be abstracted to all situations. What is at stake is who we are, how we should live our lives, and how we should act in the world.

Dharma is a key term for understanding the *Gita* and for understanding Hinduism generally. Guidance and rules for how a community should organize itself and how individuals should act and conduct themselves were contained in ancient scriptures. These scriptures, known collectively as the *Veda* ("knowledge"), were thought to be revelations from a higher source beyond this world. For many years the *Veda* was not written down but orally received and transmitted through the generations. In time this body of literature came to be regarded as *shruti*—that which has been heard by the ancient sages who communicated this revelation to humanity. Another group of later texts about conduct came to be known as that which is remembered, *smriti*, the traditions of human, although inspired, authorship. If *shruti* constitutes a primary revelation of a higher reality—some maintaining it to be a revelation from God, others simply an eternal revelation without origin—then *smriti* is a secondary revelation. *Shruti* has more authority than *smriti* but, practically, guidance about how society should conduct itself is found in the *smriti* literature, especially the law books or *Dharmashastra*.

The *Mahabharata* was thought to be composed by the sage Vyasa, and so the *Bhagavad Gita* is technically *smriti*. It is, however, for all practical purposes regarded as a revelation of God and is treated as though it were on a par with the *Veda*. It is to the *smriti* texts that we need to refer primarily to find out about the practicalities of *dharma* since they contain prescriptions for life-cycle rituals (birth, marriage, death) and statements about a person's duty with regard to their social status or class (*varna*), whether one is a priest, warrior, commoner, or servant, and stage of life, whether one is a student of the *Veda*, a householder, retired person, or renouncer. A person's "own duty" or *svadharma* varies at different stages of life and in different social groups. *Dharma* has variability depending on context. For Arjuna, his *svadharma* as a warrior or *kshatriya* is to fight in the battle as the battle is righteous.

Arjuna's moral dilemma is deeply serious. He is a warrior, and so his duty is to wage righteous war; however, his intuitive reaction is that killing his kinsfolk is wrong. He sees his teachers and relatives ranged against him on the Kauravas' side as it is their duty to serve Duryodhana, but he has doubts about the ethics of killing them in war. Even though the desires for victory and kingdom are legitimate for a warrior, in Arjuna's mind they are superseded by the virtue of peace and duty toward the family (*kuladharma*). His desire for the prosperity of the family, which would be compromised by killing his kinfolk, overrules any desire of the warrior for victory and the prosperity of the kingdom that the Pandavas will attain. The family above all needs to be preserved and upheld against lawlessness (1.40–42).

Should he therefore simply give up the world and seek salvation? What is the righteous or dharmic way to act, given the person he is? And there is more at stake than simply Arjuna's own inclinations. There is a broader ethical concern that the correct line of royal succession be established, for the Kauravas seem to have disrupted the legitimacy of this lineage. Should one group forcefully take over control and thereby challenge the established authority? As the *Gita* unfolds, Krishna responds to Arjuna's dilemma and shows him the reasons why he needs to act as a warrior in the battle and why his action is fundamentally virtuous; indeed, not to act in the way he should as *dharma* prescribes would be the opposite of virtue, it would be *adharma*.

In their dialogue, Krishna reasons with Arjuna, presenting him with a number of arguments why he should fight in the battle. This reasoning is linked to the revelation of Krishna himself as God and the approach to God through devotion (*bhakti*). Arjuna's gradual realization of the true nature of his charioteer is also his gradual persuasion about his duty and how he should act. Krishna first makes the point that Arjuna would seem like a coward, a eunuch, were he not to fight; it would be unmanly for a warrior to reject his station, and people would scorn him. It is a virtue for the warrior to fight and to place responsibility toward the broader body politic and social values over responsibility to the family alone. Arjuna's own responsibility, his *svadharma*, is to act as a noble warrior and not seem to be a coward.

Then Krishna tries to persuade Arjuna through a more philosophical argument about the self and the world. The world and person appear to be permanent and real, yet from an absolute perspective they are not. We have an underlying soul, the *atman*, which is beyond change, but everything else is in flux. Thus, while the bodies of warriors die, the soul goes on unchanging, reincarnated into body after body, as a man might discard old clothes and put on new ones (2.22), until freed from the endless cycle. It is possible only to kill the body, but the self cannot be killed; the wise, for whom happiness and suffering are the same, know this (2.15). Indeed, Arjuna should stop complaining and fight, as even if he were to die himself, this would be a doorway into heaven (2.31, 2.37). Thus he needs to develop the power of discrimination that will free him from the bond of action and its consequence (2.39). This power of discrimination the *Gita* refers to as *buddhi yoga* (2.49; 10.10; 18.57), the practice of distinguishing the true Self from what is not the Self, namely, matter or nature.

Yet still Arjuna does not fully understand why he should fight if discriminative wisdom is better than action (3.1), and if he can avoid the fight through renunciation. From chapter 3, the text develops a theological response to Arjuna's dilemma. While it is true that the wise person should cultivate an inner evenness with regard to life and death, for the soul is immortal, this does not mean that giving up the world by becoming a renouncer or mendicant is the answer. In what at first might seem to be a divergence from the main question, Krishna expounds ideas found in the ancient philosophical school of Samkhya, which claims that there are two principal realities in the universe: the individual Self (*purusha*) and nature or matter (*prakriti*). In this philosophy, the Self needs to free itself from the bonds of matter (or realize that it was, in fact, never bound). The manifest universe that we experience is within the category of matter, with action as a fundamental quality. Indeed, we might say that action is fundamental to the very nature of the universe, and the *Gita* tells us that it is the creative power that brings the universe into being (8.3), and so Arjuna cannot help but act.

But does this mean that Arjuna must inevitably be controlled by action? No, he can renounce not action itself but the results or fruits of action. He can become detached from the consequences of his acts, and so long as he acts from *dharma*, he will not suffer bad consequences. He can be *in* the world through action but not *of* the world through detachment. Not only acting with impunity, more than simply being detached from the results of action, Arjuna must hand over the fruits of action to Krishna. Act from *dharma* with detachment and God will take care of the rest. The *Gita* seems to be saying that we cannot know the consequences of our actions, although we have to act as virtue demands; but we must act with detachment in order to practice wisdom. Acting in such a way that one is detached from the consequences of action is superior to the attempted detachment from action itself (5.2).

Performing unattached action and handing over the fruits of those acts to God is an act of devotion (*bhakti*). It is here that we find the solution to Arjuna's dilemma. Because of attachment and delusion, Arjuna cannot see that his duty as a warrior is higher than his inclination toward preserving peace, and that action when performed with detachment and the spirit of devotion can itself lead toward liberation. This is what the *Gita* calls *karma yoga* (the yoga of action) (3.7): the practice of detached action rooted in virtue in which the results of that action are surrendered to God. But along with detachment from the fruits of action and surrendering the results of action to God, we also have devotion.

Although the text only uses the term *bhakti yoga* (the yoga of devotion) once (14.26), devotion to a theistic reality or God is undoubtedly the central thrust of the text and the ultimate solution to Arjuna's moral problem. The supreme verse of the *Gita* is 18.66 (known as the *carama shloka*), which says that Arjuna—and so, *mutatis mutandis*, all of us—should abandon duty and dedicate himself to Krishna, who will release him from all evils. Salvation comes from devotion to God, who will liberate us through His grace. In the *Gita*, God is a being who relates directly to us, who comes down to meet us through Krishna the king and charioteer. Indeed, from chapter 4, Krishna begins to reveal his divine nature to Arjuna. He is not simply a man like others but descended from a lineage of spiritual teachers and is of high yogic attainment, remembering all his past births and being born, not due to action (*karma*) as Arjuna was, but due to his own volition and his magical power (*maya*) (4.6). His ability to use material creation as a means to manifest himself shows that Krishna is the supreme deity, the highest God, who controls the universe. He manifests himself in times of trouble when virtue (*dharma*) is on the decline (4.7). Although the text does not use the terms "incarnation" or "descent" (*avatara*), which were to become popular later in the traditions of the god Vishnu, this is a clear indication that Krishna appears in the world for the sake of righteousness or, more specifically, to correct teachings that have decayed over time.

Anyone who understands that Krishna is God, that his birth and action (*karma*) are divine, is not reborn but goes to Krishna (4.9). Liberation (*moksha*) from the cycle of reincarnation (*samsara*), driven by action (*karma*), is thus inseparably linked to a person's perception of, and experience of, God. The chapters that follow reveal the nature of this one God who manifests himself in the world. This revelation culminates in chapter 11, when Arjuna tells Krishna that his doubts have been dispelled and his mind is now clear. He then asks Krishna to show himself in his divine form (11.1–3) and Krishna gives Arjuna a divine eye (11.8) to allow himself to be seen.

Krishna reveals himself as containing the universe, as creating and destroying all worlds and all the beings that inhabit those worlds (11.10–13). In the text Arjuna is awestruck and trembles with amazement, begging Krishna to return to his human form (11.45). This picture of a majestic Lord of the Universe, who is time itself and in whom all beings have their foundation, being, and destruction, is not the end of the matter. Krishna, upon returning to human form, avows that Arjuna is profoundly dear to him (18.64–66), revealing the secret that the deity and devotee are intimately close and that God is not only a majestic, terrifying vision but a loving companion as well. The *Gita* ends with Arjuna assuring Krishna that he has indeed been persuaded away from his initial doubts about the war, and that he will perform his warrior's duty, as he should. The next book of the *Mahabharata* opens with Arjuna preparing for war.

Historical Context

Whether or not there was a great internecine war on India's northern plains in the ancient past is impossible to say for certain, although given what we know of human societies it is possible and even probable; but there is no evidence external to the *Mahabharata* itself that could bear witness to it. Yet the theme of the war provides a narrative frame within which different doctrines, tensions, and dilemmas are worked out and brought together in a synthesis. In spite of its universal appeal, the *Bhagavad Gita* is very much a text of its time and reflects the sociopolitical and religious reality of South Asia from the cusp of the first millennium BC to the first millennium AD. In it we see ideas about kingship, sacrifice, renunciation, the nature of society as a whole, and the resolution of tensions between different paths through life, namely, ascetic renunciation and living in the world with its demands.

With the *Gita* we have one of the very earliest expressions in the history of Indian religious literature of a God, called Krishna in the text, who not only pervades the cosmos but also transcends it and stands outside it as its origin and foundation. This idea of God was modeled in part on the idea of the King. The ideal King was not a despot but administered justice and protected his people. The ideal King would defend righteousness, uphold the law (*dharma*), and display prowess in battle. In a similar vein, Krishna in the *Gita* is like a king. He is majestic and rules his kingdom, in this case the entire universe, with justice and compassion. In later traditions of the medieval period, this idea of Krishna as king comes to be replaced by Krishna as friend and lover, and we can see the beginnings of this development here when Krishna speaks of his devotees as dear (12.14–20) and tells Arjuna how dear he is to him (18.65).

At the time of the *Gita*'s composition, the religious beliefs and practices of the highest class or caste, the Brahmins, were focused on sacrifice to different gods of the earth, atmosphere, and sky to achieve benefit for the sacrificer in the next life. This sacrificial religion was being challenged by new developments, particularly by devotion to a personal God; and while the practice of sacrificial killing was disparaged, the idea or metaphor of sacrifice is central to the *Gita*. Rather than acceptance of the orthodox religion, we have a reinterpretation of sacrifice. Sacrifice is not the literal killing of animals to appease a deity, but a personal renunciation. The devotee dedicates or sacrifices his life to Krishna, inwardly renouncing the fruits of action and giving them to Krishna. Indeed, the entire epic battle can be seen as a sacrifice to righteousness.

The *Bhagavad Gita* arguably represents a reaction against the orthodox religion of the Brahmins, offering as a substitute a form of religion based on worship of a personal deity or Lord. This religion of devotion is more inclusive than the older sacrificial religion. Indeed, anyone of any social standing, including women and persons of low castes, can approach God through devotion and be accepted. The term *Bhagavan* or Lord (from which the word *Bhagavad* is derived) reflects the idea of a personal deity who is the focus of worship for a group of devotees. These devotees were known as *Bhagavatas*—those who worship *Bhagavan*. This *Bhagavan* comes to be known as Krishna, although he has synonyms, and through a complex historical process, Krishna comes to be assimilated with Vishnu (who first appears in the ancient Vedic texts). The *Gita* is a text focused on Krishna, who is the transcendent reality, and although Vishnu is mentioned three times (10.21, 11.24, and 11.30), it is clearly Krishna who is regarded as supreme. In the new kind of religion that the *Gita* reflects, the way to salvation comes about through devotion and by worshipping a personal God who transcends the universe while yet pervading it. While the *Bhagavad Gita* can be seen as a text of the *Bhagavatas*, it was nevertheless composed as an integral part of the *Mahabharata* and came to transcend any sectarian origin.

So, at the time of its composition, we have an orthodox religion of the Brahmins practicing sacrifice to deities while upholding the law and adhering to a social structure in which there were principally four social groups: the priests, or Brahmins; the warriors, or *Kshatriyas*; the commoners, or *Vaishyas*; and the serfs, or *Shudras*. The Brahmins also maintained an ideology of four stages of life: a student stage in which the *Vedas* were studied; a householder stage in which a man experienced married life and reared children; a "wilderness dweller" stage, which is in effect retirement to focus on religious duties; and a renouncer stage, in which a man leaves home to seek liberation from the cycle of reincarnation. The *Gita* reflects a rise in the importance of the *Kshatriya* class that we see in the focus on Arjuna and from the context of the broader epic, and reflects the development of devotion (*bhakti*) to a personal God. In this text, that God is Krishna, although in other traditions of Hinduism it would be a different deity, particularly Shiva and his traditions, which have a distinct literary inheritance.

Alongside the orthodox Brahminical religion and the devotionalism of groups like the *Bhagavatas*, we have the development of traditions that reject the *Veda*, particularly Buddhism and Jainism. These groups were collectively known as *Shramanas*, and are characterized by renunciation and asceticism, as well as by the belief that salvation lies beyond the world of human action and transaction. To achieve liberation, one must refrain from action that creates consequences which keep a person bound in a cycle of rebirth. Both the Buddhists and the Jains were atheistic, monastic adherents, who sought liberation through giving up the householder life, refraining from ritual action, practicing meditation, and ultimately, for Jainism, refraining from any action whatsoever in the experience of ritual death for extreme ascetics. The *Bhagavad Gita* was composed at a time when all these groups were vying with one another for patronage, and the philosophers within each group were beginning to hold sophisticated arguments with each other that endured for generations into the medieval period. The *Gita* itself rejects the Buddhist and Jain path of non-action, emphasizing instead the renunciation of the fruits of action. One can be a householder and act in the world to fulfill *dharma*, but what matters is the inner renunciation, not the outer renunciation of the mendicant groups. Similarly, the *Gita* reinterprets the orthodox religion of the Brahmins, advocating an inner sacrifice to a personal God and the sacrifice of personal desire for a higher good.

As time passed, the *Gita* came to be a very important text, especially for the followers of the religion of Vishnu and its philosophical expression in the Vedanta tradition. Because it is multilayered and rich, it is open to different interpretations. The Vedanta school of philosophy regarded the *Gita* as one of its main textual authorities, along with the *Upanishads* and *Brahma Sutras*, but they interpreted it in different ways. Shankara (AD 788–820) wrote the first commentary on the text and read the *Gita* as supporting his monistic philosophy that the individual self (*atman*) and the absolute (*Brahman*) are one. Other commentaries followed, most importantly that of Ramanuja (c. 1017–1137), who interpreted the *Gita* to mean that God is the inner controller of all things and maintained some distinction between self and God. Madhva (in the thirteenth century) thought that the text supported his own strictly dualistic theology, that the Self and God are wholly different from each other.

The *Gita* has never been particularly central to the religions of Shiva, although the famous Shaiva philosopher Abhinavagupta (c. 975–1025) wrote a commentary on the Kashmir recension, and there is also a commentary on the established text by the Shaiva Rajanaka Ramakantha (c. 950–1025). Swami Vivekananda (1863–1902) emphasized three paths taken from the *Gita* of *karma yoga*, *jnana* (knowledge) *yoga*, and *bhakti* (devotion) *yoga*, although, as we have seen, the text does not systematically expound these (indeed, the terms *jnana* and *bhakti yoga* are only mentioned at 3.3 and 14.26). Mohatma Gandhi took up the *Gita* as an important influence on his life, which he first read in Edwin Arnold's English translation, and thought it central to his message of non-violence. The *Gita* continues to hold sway over multitudes far beyond its original context and continent.

A Note on This Translation

We have used the standard version of the *Bhagavad Gita* in S. K. Belvarkar, ed., *The Mahabharata*, vol. 7, *The Bhishmaparvan* (Poona: Bhandarkar Oriental Research Institute, 1947) pp. 114–88.

Because the *Bhagavad Gita* is both a profound religious text and a great poem written in Sanskrit, our intent from the first has been twofold: to represent it in English with as great a fidelity as we could muster; and to respond to it with a poem in English. The *Gita* is a metrical composition, and we felt that we would have to find a responsive metrical arrangement for it.

The principal meter of the *Bhagavad Gita* is called the *shloka*. The *shloka* stanza is usually arranged as a couplet: two lines of sixteen syllables each. Each of these lines can be divided into two quarter verses of eight syllables each, and each of these into two metrical feet of four syllables each. *Shloka* meter is therefore syllabic, but, like the meters of classical Greek and Latin verse, it is also quantitative: that is to say, it is based on length of syllable. A syllable in the *shloka* meter is short if it contains a short vowel, long if it contains a long vowel, a diphthong, or a short vowel followed by two or more consonants, not necessarily in the same word. The patterns generated by the arrangement of long and short syllables are counterpointed by an unvarying accentual meter—trochaic tetrameter—a pattern recognizable to readers of Philip Larkin's "The Explosion":

> *On the day of the explosion*
> *Shadows pointed towards the pithead* . . .

The only other meter used by the Gita poet is *tristubh*, a stanza composed of four lines of eleven syllables each, similar to the hendecasyllabic meter of classical Greek and Latin poetry. The *tristubh* meter was used sparingly: it does not appear in every chapter and often appears by itself or in groups of two or three stanzas. The general consensus is that it was employed either for metrical variety or for emotional intensity. Interestingly, the greatest sustained use of the *tristubh* meter occurs in chapter 11, during Krishna's revelation of his divinity to Arjuna.

We decided to retain the syllabic constraints of the original. Our ideal was to restrict each of our stanzas to thirty-two syllables, and we did so for the most part, arranging them in four octosyllabic lines. Occasionally we allowed a line of nine syllables where this could be justified either by elision or creative accounting. (In our defense, it should be noted that syllabification in English is not an exact science, and that both John Milton and John Wesley treated "heaven" as a monosyllable.) We did not follow either the quantitative or qualitative rules of the *Gita*, but attempted, as we moved from a very literal prose version into verse, to find a cadence similar to that of the original. The *shloka* meter tends to divide the stanza into two symmetrical halves on the sixteenth syllable, and, for the most part, we followed this pattern. Our approach can be described as analogous rather than imitative, and we attempted to translate not word for word or line for line, but stanza for stanza.

We have retained and whenever possible deployed the heroic epithets that Krishna and Arjuna employ throughout the *Gita*, as they illustrate the great love and admiration that these two have for each other, and they help to give us a sense of the flavor of that society the *Gita* was written about— archaic, heroic, and on the edge of its catastrophic doom.

One of the issues involved in translating the *Gita* stems from the recognition that, in rendering Sanskrit words into English, we inevitably reduce the semantic range of terms such as *dharma, atman*, and *guna*. This is true, but we have felt that the reader without Sanskrit would be at a greater disadvantage faced with the untranslated terms than with an admittedly partial account in English. We also felt it as part of our duty (*dharma*, in this case) to bring the work over into English, whatever its limitations as a language or ours as translators.

We wish to thank the editors of *Blackbird* and *Eleven Eleven*, in which portions of this work have previously appeared.

We are grateful to Robert Hass and to Daniel Gold and Vinay Dharwadker, who read our work and gave us thoughtful and useful comments about it. At Norton, we have benefited from the care of Ann Adelman. Our greatest thanks must go to our editor, Carol Bemis, who first suggested this project to us, and to her assistant, Rivka Genesen, for their ongoing dedication and support.

THE
BHAGAVAD GITA

chapter

1

Dhritarashtra said,

"Having gathered, battle-hungry   1
on virtue's field, the field of Kuru,
what did they do then, Sanjaya,
my sons and the sons of Pandu?"

Sanjaya said,

"King Duryodhana, witnessing   2
the army of the Pandavas
drawn up in battle lines, approached
his teacher and said this to him:

'Master, observe this enormous   3
army of the sons of Pandu
deployed for battle by your wise
pupil, the son of Drupada!

'Here are heroes, mighty archers,   4
Bhima's equal, Arjuna's too,
Yuyudhana and Virata,
with mighty Drupada himself;

'Dhrishtaketu, Chekitana,   5
and the noble king of Kashis,
Purujit and Kuntibhoga,
and Shaibya, that human bull;

'Great-spirited Yudhamanyu   6
and valorous Uttamauja;
Subhadra's son, Draupadi's sons;
all are great warriors indeed!

'O best of all who are twice-born,   7
I shall now list the names for you
of our most distinguished men,
the leaders by whom we are led:

'Your Lordship first, and then Bhishma,   8
Karna and triumphant Kripa;
Ashvatthaman and Vikarna,
and Somadatta's son as well,

'and many other heroes who   9
are here prepared to die for me;
all battle-hardened warriors,
and all of them diversely armed.

'Our army, under Bhishma,   10
is the equal of their forces;
the enemy, protected by
Bhima, is not a match for us.

'So, wherever you are stationed   11
in your true place along the line,
your Lordships all must remember,
Bhishma is to be protected!'

"Like a lion, Bhishma bellowed,   12
That wise old man of the Kurus,
and blew his conch, full of power,
bringing joy to Duryodhana!

"Then conches and the kettledrums,   13
the cymbals, drums and trumpets too,
all at once indeed were sounded
in a tumultuous uproar!

"Standing in their great chariot   14
drawn by a yoked pair of white steeds,
Krishna and the Son of Pandu
blew upon their sacred conches:

"Lord Krishna blew 'The Demon's Horn,'   15
and Arjuna blew 'Heaven's Gift';
wolf-bellied Bhima, fierce in war,
blew upon the great conch 'Paundra.'

"Kunti's son, King Yudhishthira,   16
blew the conch 'Endless Victory';
Nakula and Sahadeva blew
'Sweet of Tone' and 'Jewel-Flowered.'

"The Kashis' king, best of archers,   17
Shikandi, that great warrior,
Dhrishtadyumna and Virata,
Satyaki, the invincible,

"in unison, O Dhritarashtra,   18
with the fierce son of Subhadra,
Drupada and Draupadi's sons
blew their conches respectively:

"rolling as it did like thunder   19
between the earth and firmament,
that great commotion caused the hearts
of Dhritarashtra's sons to burst!

"Now Monkey-Bannered Arjuna,   20
seeing his foes drawn up for war,
raised his bow, that Son of Pandu,
as the weapons began to clash.

"Then he said these words to Krishna: 21
'Lord of the Earth, Unshaken One,
bring my chariot to a halt
between the two adverse armies,

'so I may see these men, arrayed   22
here for the battle they desire,
whom I am soon to undertake
a warrior's delight in fighting!

'I see those who have assembled,   23
the warriors prepared to fight,
eager to perform in battle
for Dhritarashtra's evil son!'

"When Arjuna had spoken so   24
to Krishna, O Bharata,
he, having brought their chariot
to a halt between the armies,

"in the face of Bhisma, Drona,   25
and the other Lords of the Earth,
said, 'Behold, O Son of Pritha,
how these Kurus have assembled!'

"And there the Son of Pritha saw   26
rows of grandfathers and grandsons;
sons and fathers, uncles, in-laws;
teachers, brothers and companions,

"all relatives and friends of his   27
in both of the assembled armies.
And seeing them arrayed for war,
Arjuna, the Son of Kunti,

"felt for them a great compassion,   28
as well as great despair, and said,
'O Krishna, now that I have seen
my relatives so keen for war,

'I am unstrung: my limbs collapse   29
beneath me, and my mouth is dry,
there is a trembling in my body,
and my hair rises, bristling;

'Gandiva, my immortal bow,   30
drops from my hand and my skin burns,
I cannot stand upon my feet,
my mind rambles in confusion—

'All inauspicious are the signs   31
that I see, O Handsome-Haired One!
I foresee no good resulting
from slaughtering my kin in war!

'I have no wish for victory,   32
nor for kingship and its pleasures!
O Krishna, what good is kingship?
What good even life and pleasure?

'Those for whose sake we desire   33
kingship, pleasures and enjoyments,
are now drawn up in battle lines,
their lives and riches now abandoned:

'fathers, grandfathers; sons, grandsons;   34
my mother's brothers and the men
who taught me in my youth; brothers-
and fathers-in-law: kinsmen all!

'Though they are prepared to slay us,   35
I do not wish to murder them,
not even to rule the three worlds—
how much less one earthly kingdom?

'What joy for us in murdering   36
Dhritarashtra's sons, O Krishna?
for if we killed these murderers,
evil like theirs would cling to us!

'So we cannot in justice slay   37
our kinsmen, Dhritarashtra's sons,
for, having killed our people, how
could we be pleased, O Madhava?

'Even if they, mastered by greed,   38
are blind to the consequences
of the family's destruction,
of friendships lost to treachery,

'how are we not to comprehend 39
that we must turn back from evil?
The wrong done by this destruction
is evident, O Shaker of Men.

'For with the family destroyed, 40
its eternal laws must perish;
and when they perish, lawlessness
overwhelms the whole family.

'Whelmed by lawlessness, the women 41
of the family are corrupted;
from corrupted women comes
the intermingling of classes.

'Such intermingling sends to hell 42
the family and its destroyers:
their ancestors fall then, deprived
of rice and water offerings.

'Those who destroy the family, 43
who institute class mingling,
cause the laws of the family
and laws of caste to be abolished.

'Men whose familial laws have been 44
obliterated, O Krishna,
are damned to dwell eternally
in hell, as we have often heard.

'It grieves me that as we intend   45
to murder our relatives
in our greed for pleasures, kingdoms,
we are fixed on doing evil!

'If the sons of Dhritarashtra,   46
armed as they are, should murder me
weaponless and unresisting,
I would know greater happiness!'

"And having spoken, Arjuna   47
collapsed into his chariot,
his bow and arrows clattering,
and his mind overcome with grief."

chapter

2

Sanjaya said,

"Said Madhu-Slaying Krishna to   1
Arjuna, whose downcast eyes
were brimming over, overcome
by pity mingled with despair:

   "The Lord said,

'Where has it come from, Arjuna,   2
your weakness in a testing time,
so unsuited to one highborn?
Disgrace, not heaven, is its end!

'O Son of Pritha, impotence   3
does not become your true nature!
Abandon your faintheartedness,
rise up, O Scorcher of the Foe!'

  "Arjuna said,

'How can I possibly make war   4
against those venerable men,
Bhisma and Drona, with my bow,
O Slayer of the Demon Madhu?

'Sooner would I go begging for my dinner   5
than ever slay those worthiest of teachers;
if I slew them, although they wish my kingdom,
my dinner would be stained with bloody carnage.

'Nor do we know whether it would be better   6
for us to vanquish them or be overcome.
We would not wish to live on after slaying
the sons of Dhritarashtra here before us.

'The flaw of pity overcomes my being,   7
my mind is too confused to know its duty;
tell me for certain, which of these is better?
Instruct the student who prostrates himself before you!

'Nothing I see can remedy the sorrow   8
that has completely withered all my senses,
not if I had unrivaled earthly power,
not if I had authority in heaven!'

Sanjaya said,

"Thus Arjuna, the Thick-Haired One,   9
to Krishna, the Divine Cowherd:
'I will not fight.' And nothing more
did he say after saying that.

"Then Krishna, the Unshaken One,   10
addressed dejected Arjuna
as they stood between the armies,
while laughing at him, as it were:

"The Lord said:

'Although you seem to speak wisely,   11
you have mourned those not to be mourned:
the wise do not grieve for those gone
or for those who are not yet gone.

'There was no time when I was not,   12
nor you, nor these lords around us,
and there will never be a time
henceforth when we shall not exist.

'The embodied one passes through   13
childhood, youth, and then old age,
then attains another body;
in this the wise are undeceived.

'Contacts with matter by which we   14
feel heat and cold, pleasure and pain,
are transitory, come and go:
these you must manage to endure.

'Such contacts do not agitate   15
a wise man, O Bull among Men,
to whom pleasure and pain are one.
He is fit for immortality.

'Non-being cannot come to be,   16
nor can what *is* come to be not.
The certainty of these sayings
is known by seers of the truth.

'Know it as indestructible,   17
that by which all is pervaded;
no one may cause the destruction
of the imperishable one.

'Bodies of the embodied one,   18
eternal, boundless, all-enduring,
are said to die; the one cannot:
therefore, take arms, O Bharata!

'This man believes the one may kill;   19
That man believes it may be killed;
both of them lack understanding:
it can neither kill nor *be* killed.

'It is not born, nor is it ever mortal,   20
and having been, will not pass from existence;
ancient, unborn, eternally existing,
it does not die when the body perishes.

'How can a man who knows the one   21
to be eternal (both unborn
and without end) murder or cause
another to? Whom does he kill?

'Someone who has abandoned worn-out
        garments   22
sets out to clothe himself in brand-new raiment;
just so, when it has cast off worn-out bodies,
the embodied one will encounter others.

'This may not be pierced by weapons,   23
nor can this be consumed by flames;
flowing waters cannot drench this,
nor blowing winds desiccate this.

'Not to be pierced, not to be burned,   24
neither drenched nor desiccated—
eternal, all-pervading, firm,
unmoving, everlasting this!

'This has been called unmanifest,   25
unthinkable and unchanging;
therefore, because you know this now,
you should not lament, Arjuna.

'But even if you think that this   26
is born and dies time after time,
forever, O great warrior,
not even then should you mourn this.

'Death is assured to all those born,   27
and birth assured to all the dead;
you should not mourn what is merely
inevitable consequence.

'Beginnings are unmanifest,   28
but manifest the middle-state,
and ends unmanifest again;
so what is your complaint about?

'Somebody looks upon this as a marvel,   29
and likewise someone tells about this marvel,
and yet another hears about this marvel,
but even having heard it, no one knows it.

'The one cannot ever perish   30
in a body it inhabits,
O Descendant of Bharata;
and so no being should be mourned.

'Nor should you tremble to perceive   31
your duty as a warrior;
for him there is nothing better
than a battle that is righteous.

'And if by chance they will have gained   32
the wide open gate of heaven,
O Son of Pritha, warriors
rejoice in fighting such as that!

'If you turn from righteous warfare,   33
your behavior will be evil,
for you will have abandoned both
your duty and your honored name.

'People will speak of your disgrace   34
forever, and an honored man
who falls from honor into shame
suffers a fate much worse than death.

'Great warriors will think you've turned   35
away from battle's joy in fear;
and those who once thought well of you
will think you insignificant.

'Unspeakable words will be said   36
about you by your enemies!
Your prowess will be ridiculed!
What greater suffering than that?

'If slain, you will attain heaven;   37
victorious, the earth is yours!
Therefore, rise up, O Son of Kunti,
be resolute for the battle!

'When pleasure is the same as pain,   38
profit as loss, conquest, defeat,
then join the battle, Arjuna;
evil will not be heaped on you!

'Theory proclaims the higher mind,   39
but hear of it in practice now.
Yoked by the higher mind, you will
give up being bound by action.

'Here there is no loss of effort,   40
no backsliding, Son of Pritha;
just a little of this yoga
will protect one from great danger.

'Here higher mind, so resolute,   41
is undivided, Arjuna,
though minds of the irresolute
branch out in many endless ways.

'The undiscerning, whose delight   42
is in the Vedic ritual,
utter florid speech, proclaiming,
"Why, there is nothing else but this!"

'Those whose nature is desire,   43
fixed on heaven, turn to varied
rituals of lust and power,
the fruit of which will be rebirth.

'Their meditation does not grant   44
a resolute intelligence
to those attached to lust and power,
whose thought is stolen by their speech.

'Nature is the *Vedas*' subject;   45
be free of the three qualities,
Arjuna, and the opposing pairs:
abide in truth, possessed of self.

'What is the purpose of a well   46
overflowing on every side?
Just as useful are the *Vedas*
for the knowledgeable Brahmin.

'Your concern should be with action,   47
never with an action's fruits;
these should never motivate you,
nor attachment to inaction.

'Established in this practice, act   48
without attachment, Arjuna,
unmoved by failure or success!
Equanimity is yoga.

'Action is far inferior   49
to the practice of higher mind;
seek refuge there, for pitiful
are those moved by fruit of action!

'One disciplined by higher mind   50
here casts off good and bad actions;
therefore, be yoked to discipline;
discipline is skill in actions.

'Having left the fruit of action,   51
the wise ones yoked to higher mind
are freed from the bonds of rebirth,
and go where no corruption is.

'When your higher mind has crossed   52
over the thicket of delusion,
you will become disenchanted
with what is heard in the *Vedas*.

'When, unvexed by revelation,   53
your higher mind is motionless
and stands fixed in meditation,
then you will attain discipline.'

"Arjuna asked,

'Tell me, Krishna, how may I know   54
the man steady in his wisdom,
who abides in meditation?
How should that one sit, speak and move?'

"The Blessed Lord replied,

'When he renounces all desires   55
entering his mind, Arjuna,
and his self rests within the Self,
then his wisdom is called steady.

'He who is not agitated   56
by suffering or by desires,
freed from anger, fear and passions,
is called a sage of steady mind.

'Who is wholly unimpassioned,   57
not rejoicing in the pleasant,
nor rejecting the unpleasant,
is established in his wisdom.

'And when this one wholly withdraws   58
all his senses from their objects,
as a tortoise draws in its limbs,
his wisdom is well-established.

'When the embodied one abstains   59
from food, sense-objects disappear,
save for flavor, which will depart
after one beholds the highest.

'And yet the agitated senses   60
even of the discerning man
who strives against them, Arjuna,
will carry off his mind by force.

'He who has subdued his senses,   61
should sit, controlled, intent on me.
The wisdom of one whose senses
are subdued is well-established.

'Attachment to sense-objects comes   62
to one who meditates on them;
from attachment comes desire,
and from desire, anger comes.

'Delusion rises out of anger,   63
loss of mindfulness from delusion;
with mindfulness gone, higher mind
perishes, and the man is lost.

'One unyoked to hates and passions,   64
though engaging with sense-objects,
is self-controlled and self-restrained.
That one attains tranquility.

'Cessation of all suffering   65
is born of his tranquility.
The intellect at once becomes
steady for one of tranquil thought.

'There is no higher mind in one   66
without control, nor meditation;
no peace without meditation;
and without peace, no happiness.

'The mind that regulates itself   67
by the undisciplined senses
loses discernment, as the wind
blows a ship from its course at sea.

'Therefore, O Strong-Armed Warrior,   68
he whose senses have been withdrawn
from sense-objects is said to be
well-established in his wisdom.

'In the nighttime of all beings,   69
the self-controlled man is awake;
that time when beings are awake
is nighttime for the seeing sage.

'For just as waters pour into the ocean,   70
which, when it fills, becomes still and unmoving,
peace comes to one whom all desires enter,
not to the one who still desires desires.

'The man who has abandoned all   71
desire moves, free from longing,
indifferent to "me" and "mine,"
and without ego, attains peace.

'This is the divine condition;   72
who, undeluded, comes to this,
abiding there till his end-time,
Arjuna, knows the absolute.'"

chapter

3

"Arjuna said:

'If you regard the intellect   1
as superior to action,
why urge me, O Handsome-Haired One,
into actions so appalling?

'By your equivocating speech   2
my mind is, as it were, confused.
Tell me this one thing, and clearly:
By what means may I reach the best?'

"The Blessed Lord said:

'As I have previously taught,   3
there are two paths, O Blameless One:
there is the discipline of knowledge
and the discipline of action.

'Not by not acting in this world   4
does one become free from action,
nor does one approach perfection
by renunciation only.

'Not even for a moment does   5
someone exist without acting.
Even against one's will, one acts
by the nature-born qualities.

'He who has restrained his senses,   6
but sits and summons back to mind
the sense-objects, is said to be
a self-deluding hypocrite.

'But he whose mind controls his senses,   7
who undertakes the discipline
of action by the action-organs,
without attachment, is renowned.

'You must act as bid, for action   8
is better than non-action is:
not even functions of the body
could be sustained by non-action.

'This world is bound by action, save   9
for action which is sacrifice;
therefore, O Son of Kunti, act
without attachment to your deeds.

'When Prajapati brought forth life,   10
he brought forth sacrifice as well,
saying, "By this may you produce,
may this be your wish-fulfilling cow."

'Nourish the gods with sacrifice,   11
and they will nourish you as well.
By nourishing each other, you
will realize the highest good.

'Nourished by sacrifice, the gods   12
will give the pleasures you desire.
One who enjoys such gifts without
repaying them is just a thief.

'The good, who eat of the remains   13
from sacrifice, rise up faultless.
But the wicked, who cook only
for their own sakes, eat their own filth.

'Beings come to exist by food,   14
which emanates from the rain god,
who comes to be by sacrifice,
which arises out of action.

'Know that action comes from Brahman,   15
Brahman comes from the eternal;
so the all-pervading Brahman
is based in sacrifice forever.

'One who in this world does not turn   16
the wheel, thus setting it in motion,
lives uselessly, O Son of Pritha,
a sensual, malicious life.

'But the man whose only pleasure   17
and satisfaction is the self,
which is his sole contentment too,
has no task he must accomplish.

'That man finds no significance   18
in what has, or has not, been done;
moreover, he does not depend
on any being whatsoever.

'Therefore, act without attachment   19
in whatever situation,
for by the practice of detached
action, one attains the highest.

'Only by action Janaka   20
and the others reached perfection.
In order to maintain the world,
your obligation is to act.

'Whatever the best leader does   21
the rank and file will also do;
everyone will fall in behind
the standard such a leader sets.

'O Son of Pritha, there is nought   22
that I need do in the three worlds,
nor anything I might attain;
and yet I take part in action.

'For if I were not always to   23
engage in action ceaselessly,
men everywhere would soon follow
in my path, O Son of Pritha.

'Should I not engage in action,   24
these worlds would perish, utterly;
I would cause a great confusion,
and destroy all living beings.

'The unwise are attached to action   25
even as they act, Arjuna;
so, for the welfare of the world,
the wise should act with detachment.

'The wise should not cause confusion   26
in the unwise, attached to action;
but by living in discipline,
bring them to enjoy all actions.

'All actions are undertaken   27
by the qualities of nature,
though one deceived by his ego
imagines, 'I am doing this.'

'Who understands the division   28
between action and quality,
and knows that qualities act on
one another, is not attached.

'Those whom the qualities deceive   29
are attached to those qualities;
Those who are all-knowing should not
agitate weak-minded dullards.

'Referring all your deeds to me,   30
and focused solely on the Self,
desireless, devoid of ego,
free of fever, join the battle!

'All those who practice constantly   31
my doctrine without grumbling
because they have had faith in me,
they are released from their actions.

'But those who whine and sneer at this   32
are not practicing my doctrine;
know such people as deluded
to all knowledge, lost and mindless.

'Even a man of wisdom acts   33
in accordance with his nature.
Since beings act in this way, what
is accomplished by suppression?

'Sensual love and hatred both   34
abide in what senses desire:
one should not submit to these two,
since their powers will block his path.

'Better to do one's own duty   35
ineptly, than another's well.
Death is better in one's duty;
another's duty invites fear.'

     "Arjuna said:

'Say what impels a man to do   36
such evil, Krishna, what great force
urges him, forces him into it,
even if he is unwilling?'

"The Blessed Lord said:

'Know that the enemy is this: 37
desire, anger, whose origins
are in the quality of passion,
all-consuming, greatly harmful.

'As fire is obscured by smoke,   38
or by dust, a mirror's surface,
or an embryo by its membrane,
so this is covered up by that.

'Knowledge is constantly obscured   39
by this enemy of the wise,
by this insatiable fire
whose form, Arjuna, is desire.

'The senses, mind, and intellect   40
are its abode, as it is said.
Having obscured knowledge with these,
it deludes the embodied one.

'When you have subdued your senses,   41
then, O Bull of the Bharatas,
kill this demon, the destroyer
of all knowledge and discernment.

'Senses are said to be important,   42
but mind is higher than they are,
and intellect is above mind;
but Self is greater than all these.

'So knowing it to be supreme,   43
and sustaining the self with Self,
slay the foe whose form is desire,
so hard to conquer, Arjuna.'"

"The Blessed Lord said:

'This is the undying yoga   1
that I proclaimed to Vivasvat,
who related it to Manu,
and Ikshvaku had it from him.

'The royal seers came to learn this   2
yoga from a long tradition;
but after many ages, it
was lost, O Scorcher of the Foe.

'I proclaim this ancient yoga   3
to you here today, Arjuna:
you are my devotee and friend,
and this is the supreme secret.'

"Arjuna said:

'But the Sun God, Vivasvat, was   4
born earlier than Your Lordship;
how may I understand that you
proclaimed this in the beginning?'

"The Blessed Lord said:

'Arjuna, you and I have had   5
many births which have passed away;
I know all of these births, but you
do not, O Scorcher of the Foe.

'Though I am unborn and deathless,   6
and the Lord of All Creation,
superior to my own nature,
I create myself by magic.

'Indeed, whenever righteousness   7
decays, O Son of Bharata,
and unrighteousness increases,
then do I manifest myself.

'In order to protect the good,   8
and to destroy evildoers,
and to establish righteousness,
age after age, I come to be.

'He who truly knows my divine   9
birth and action, Arjuna,
will not be reborn when he sheds
his body, but will come to me.

'Emptied of anger, fear and passion,   10
many men are imbued with me;
purified by austere wisdom,
they come into my condition.

'So I reward the devotion   11
of all those who resort to me;
everywhere my followers walk
in my path, O Son of Pritha.

'Seeking ritual fulfillment,   12
they offer sacrifice to gods,
for in this human world, success
born of ritual comes quickly.

'I created the four classes,   13
their different qualities and roles.
Although I am their creator,
know me as one who never acts!

'I am left unstained by actions,   14
not wishing any of their fruit;
so the one who understands me
is not fettered by his actions.

'The ancients who wished for release   15
knew this too, and so they acted.
Therefore, you must act as they did,
those who lived in earlier times.

'"So what is action and non-action?"   16
This confuses even poets.
I will tell you of this action
which will free you from corruption.

'To be enlightened, one should know   17
the way of actions, good and bad.
Non-action one should also know.
The way of action is profound.

'Who in action sees non-action,   18
and sees in non-action, action,
is a wise man, is disciplined,
whole in all actions he performs.

'In all his undertakings, he   19
ignores desire and volition.
The wise see him as wise, whose acts
have been burned in wisdom's fire.

'With no attachment to the fruit   20
of action, always satisfied,
independent, he does not act—
even when engaged in action.

'No guilt attaches to one whose   21
self is governed by his yoked mind,
and who performs, without desire,
actions only in his body.

'Content with what he gains by chance,   22
undivided, free of envy,
success and failure one to him,
he is not bound by his actions.

'The acts of one unattached and free,   23
whose consciousness dwells in knowledge,
are performed as sacrifices;
and such acts utterly dissolve.

'Brahman is offering, Brahman   24
is the oblation and the fire,
to be attained by one intent
on Brahman seen in all actions.

'Some yogis practice sacrifice   25
to a god while others offer
sacrifice by sacrificing
in the fire of the Brahman.

'Some offer senses—hearing, say—   26
into the fires of restraint;
some give sense-objects, such as sound,
to the fires of the senses.

'Others offer up all actions   27
of the senses and of the breath
to the fires of the yoga
of knowledge-kindled self-restraint.

'Others offer material things,   28
their discipline as sacrifice;
and some there are who with keen vows
sacrifice knowledge and self-study.

'Having restrained the double paths   29
of breathing in and breathing out,
and focused on control of breath,
others make this their sacrifice.

'Others who restrict consumption   30
of food offer breaths into breaths;
all these indeed know sacrifice,
which has purged their impurities.

'Who eat the leavings of the gods   31
at sacrifice go to Brahman.
This world is not for those who do
not sacrifice: how then the next?

'Many the kinds of sacrifice   32
set before the mouth of Brahman;
know that all are born of action,
and this knowledge will release you.

'Better than material sacrifice   33
is the sacrifice of knowledge:
all action is perfected by
knowledge, O Scorcher of the Foe.

'Know this, O Son of Pritha: by   34
submission, inquiry and service,
the seers of reality
will instruct you in this knowledge;

'having attained it, you will not   35
fall again into delusion,
for by it you will see all beings
first in yourself and then in me.

'Were you the very worst of all   36
the very worst of sinful men,
nonetheless, you would transcend all
evils in the boat of knowledge.

'Thus, even as a kindled fire   37
reduces firewood to ash,
the fire of knowledge, Arjuna,
acts upon all actions so.

'Nothing in this world may be found   38
that purifies as knowledge does;
one whose yoga is perfected
will find such knowledge in the Self.

'A faithful man, restrained in senses,   39
holding knowledge as highest good,
obtains it quickly; with it, he
achieves (and not unswiftly!) bliss.

'The ignorant unfaithful one   40
whose self is doubtful is destroyed.
Neither in this world nor the next,
can there be happiness for him.

'One whose actions are renounced by   41
yoga, and who is self-possessed,
with knowledge that dispels all doubt
is not bound by deeds, Arjuna.

'So, having cut away doubt, caused   42
by ignorance within the heart,
with the sword of your self-knowledge,
turn to yoga! Rise, Arjuna!'"

"Arjuna said:

'Now you praise renunciation,   1
now, O Krishna, you praise yoga:
without equivocation, say
which is the better of these two?'

"The Blessed Lord said:

'Yoga and renunciation   2
will both lead to ultimate bliss;
but the yoga of action is
better than renunciation.

'Renunciation's exemplar   3
is without hatred or desire;
indifferent to opposites,
he is lightly freed from bondage.

'Fools say, "Theory and practice   4
are different!" But not the wise:
either one performed correctly
will yield the fruit common to both.

'The place attained by theory   5
is also gotten to by practice.
Who sees that theory is one
with practice, accurately sees!

'Renunciation, Arjuna,   6
is hard to attain without yoga.
The sage, by yoga disciplined,
in no great time reaches Brahman.

'One yoked by yoga, whose cleansed self   7
and senses both have been subdued,
whose self is now that of all beings,
is untainted by his actions.

'Whether seeing, hearing, touching,   8
tasting, eating, moving, sleeping,
even breathing, "*I* do nothing,"
the yoked-by-yoga seer will say,

'speaking, letting go or grasping; 9
opening the eyes or closing,
while believing that "the senses
act so upon the sense-objects."

'One who, in acting, consecrates 10
all of his actions to Brahman,
shed of attachments, is unstained
like a lotus leaf by water.

'With body, mind and intellect, 11
even merely with the senses,
the yogis act without attachment,
so as to purify the self.

'Unattached to action's fruits, 12
the yoked one comes to final peace;
the unyoked are bound by desires
and by attachment to results.

'All actions of the mind renounced, 13
the Self embodied sits in peace
within the city of nine gates,
and neither acts nor causes action.

'The Lord is not responsible 14
for worldly acts or agency,
nor for linking act to outcome;
inherent nature causes these.

'The all-pervading has no share   15
either in evil or in good.
Knowledge is veiled by ignorance,
whereby people are deluded.

'But those whose ignorance of Self   16
is overcome by their knowledge,
find that knowledge is like the sun,
illuminating the supreme!

'Those whose minds are fixed upon it,   17
whose selves are set upon this goal,
with their impurities all cleansed
by knowledge will not be reborn.

'The wise ones see the very same   18
in a learned, cultured Brahmin,
a cow, an elephant, a dog—
or in a dog-cooking outcaste!

'They overcome creation, who   19
dwell here in equanimity:
Brahman is faultless and equable;
therefore, they abide in Brahman.

'One should not thrill at what delights, 20
nor shudder at what one abhors;
who knows the absolute, abides
in *it*—steady, undeluded.

'The self detached from externals 21
finds happiness within the Self.
One whose Self is joined to Brahman
attains undying happiness.

'Those pleasures born of touch are wombs 22
of suffering, O Son of Kunti!
Because they are contained in time,
they do not satisfy the wise.

'One who is able to endure 23
the lashings of rage and desire
before escaping from the body,
is disciplined and is content.

'With happiness and joy within, 24
and inner radiance thereby,
a yogi will indeed attain
extinction and become Brahman.

'Seers shed all of impurities, 25
with doubts dispelled and selves restrained,
benevolent to all beings,
attain extinction in Brahman.

'Ascetics separated from 26
rage and lust, of disciplined minds,
who know the self, are very close
to their extinction in Brahman.

'Excluding all external contacts,⠀⠀⠀⠀⠀27
with his gaze fixed between the brows,
with inhalations equal to
his exhalations, the wise one,

'whose senses, mind and intellect⠀⠀⠀⠀28
are firmly fixed upon release,
shed of desire, fear and rage
will soon attain bliss forever.

'Who understands me as the Friend⠀⠀⠀⠀29
of all Beings, Lord of this World,
Enjoyer of Sacrifices
and Austerities, attains peace!'"

chapter

6

"The Blessed Lord said,

'He who performs the rituals   1
without attachment to their fruits,
is a renouncer and a yogi,
not he who lacks rites and fires.

'Know, Arjuna, that what is called   2
renunciation is yoga!
For no one becomes a yogi
without renouncing volition.

'Acts are said to be the means of   3
the sage who would rise to yoga;
tranquility is called the means
of the one who has ascended.

'A man detached from his actions   4
and the objects of the senses,
who renounces all volition,
is said to have risen to yoga.

'By the Self one should raise the self,   5
but one should not degrade the self,
for the self is the Self's true friend,
and may indeed be the Self's foe.

'The self overcome by the Self   6
has the Self as its companion;
but the Self is inimical
to the self that is unsubdued.

'The supreme Self of the self-subdued   7
and tranquil one is collected
in cold, heat, pleasure and pain,
in honor and dishonor too.

'Whose self, subdued, is satisfied   8
by knowledge and insight, aloof,
and sees clods, stones and gold nuggets
as one, is said to be a yogi.

'Who sits apart, indifferent   9
to foes, associates and friends,
neutral to enemies and kinsmen,
righteous and wicked, is renowned.

'The yogi should be self-subdued   10
always, and stand in solitude,
alone, controlled in thought and self,
without desires or possessions.

'Having established for himself   11
a steady seat in a pure place,
neither too high nor yet too low,
covered with grass, deerhide and cloth,

'with his mind sharpened to one point,   12
with thought and senses both subdued,
there he should sit, doing yoga
so as to purify the self,

'keeping his head, neck and body   13
aligned, erect and motionless,
gaze fixed on the tip of his nose,
not looking off distractedly,

'now fearless and with tranquil self,   14
firm in avowed celibacy,
with his thought focused on myself,
he should sit, devoted to me.

'Thus always chastening himself   15
the yogi's mind, subdued, knows peace,
whose farthest point is cessation;
thereafter, he abides in me.

'Yoga is not for the greedy,   16
nor yet for the abstemious;
not for one too used to sleeping,
nor for the sleepless, Arjuna.

'Yoga destroys the pain of one   17
temperate in his behavior,
in his food and recreation,
and in his sleep and waking too.

'After his thought has been subdued,   18
and abides only in the Self,
free from all longing and desire,
then he is said to be steadfast.

'"Like a lamp in a windless place   19
unflickering," is the likeness
of the yogi subdued in thought,
performing yoga of the Self.

'Where all thought comes to cease, restrained   20
by the discipline of yoga,
where, by the self, the Self is seen,
one is satisfied in the Self.

'When he knows that eternal joy   21
grasped only by the intellect,
beyond the senses where he dwells,
he does not deviate from truth;

'having attained it, he believes   22
there is no gain superior;
abiding there, he is unmoved
even by profound suffering.

'Let him know that the dissolving   23
of the union with suffering
is called yoga, to be practiced
with persistence, mind undaunted.

'Having abandoned all desires   24
born to satisfy intentions,
and having utterly restrained
the many senses by the mind,

'Gradually let him find rest,   25
his intellect under control,
his mind established in the Self,
not thinking about anything.

'Having subdued the unsteady   26
mind in motion, he should lead it
back from wherever it strays to,
into the domain of the Self.

'Supreme joy comes to the yogi   27
of calm mind and tranquil passion,
who has become one with Brahman
and is wholly free of evil.

'Constantly controlling himself,   28
the yogi, freed from evil now,
swiftly attains perpetual
joy of contact here with Brahman.

'He whose self is yoked by yoga,   29
and who perceives sameness always,
will see the Self in all beings
and see all beings in the Self.

'I am not lost for someone who   30
perceives my presence everywhere,
and everything perceives in me,
nor is that person lost for me.

'The yogi firmly set in oneness   31
who worships me in all beings,
whatever the path that he takes,
will nonetheless abide in me.

'The yogi who sees all the same   32
analogous to his own Self
in happiness or suffering
is thought supreme, O Arjuna.'

"Arjuna said,

'Because of mind's unsteadiness   33
I do not see the changeless state
of the yoga known as sameness,
O Slayer of the Demon Madhu!

'Krishna, the mind is most infirm,   34
is troubling, powerful, intense!
I think it no less difficult
to subjugate than is the wind!'

"The Blessed Lord said,

'Doubtless, O Mighty Warrior,   35
the restless mind resists restraints;
but by practice, O Son of Kunti,
and by detachment, it is gripped.

'Yoga, I say, is hard to reach   36
by one whose self is unsubdued;
with effort, someone self-controlled
may find the means to attain it.'

"Arjuna said,

'One faithful, but yet unsubdued,   37
whose mind has strayed from discipline,
not having reached that perfection,
what path does he walk, O Krishna?

'Fallen from here and hereafter,   38
does he just vanish like a cloud,
fluctuating, O Great-Armed One,
baffled on the path of Brahman?

'Only you and no one other   39
can totally efface my doubts;
none but you comes forth, O Krishna,
to efface my uncertainty!'

"The Blessed Lord said,

'Neither down here nor hereafter   40
will he be found to be destroyed,
O Son of Pritha; for no one
who does good comes to a bad end.

'Having dwelled for ages in the   41
worlds of the meritorious,
one lost to yoga is reborn
in an illustrious family.

'Or else he comes to be within   42
a family of wise yogis;
but such a kind of birth as this
is hard to attain in this world.

'There he rejoins an intellect   43
drawn from a past incarnation,
and so he struggles once again,
O Joy of Kuru, for perfection.

'Even against his will, he is   44
sustained by previous practice;
he who even wishes to know
yoga transcends the Word-Brahman.

'From his striving with a conquered   45
mind, the sage, cleansed of defilement,
and purified through many births,
will pass to the supreme abode.

'The yogi is superior   46
to ascetics and the learned,
and to those who perform the rites;
so, Arjuna, be a yogi!

'Also, of all yogis, the one   47
whose inner Self has come to me,
who worships me, rich in his faith,
is thought to be the most steadfast.'"

chapter
7

"The Blessed Lord said:

'Arjuna, hear how with your mind   1
subsumed in me as your refuge,
practicing yoga, you will come
to know me wholly, without doubt!

'I will grant this knowledge fully   2
and with it give understanding,
beyond which there is nothing more
in this world that you need to know.

'Of many thousands, just a few   3
strive for perfection here below;
and of those who strive, perfected,
scarcely any know me truly.

'Earth and water, fire and wind,   4
ether, mind, intellect, ego:
this is the eightfold division
of my material nature.

'Know this as my inferior   5
nature, Arjuna; my other,
higher nature consists of souls
through which this universe abides!

'Understand my higher nature   6
as the womb of every being;
thus the source and dissolution
of the entire universe.

'There is nothing superior   7
to me, O Conqueror of Wealth;
this universe is strung on me
as pearls are strung upon a thread.

'I am water's taste, Arjuna,   8
I am the light of sun and moon,
the *Vedas'* sacred syllable,
sound in the air, manhood in men.

'I am the pure fragrance of earth   9
and the radiance of fire;
I am the life in all beings,
the ascetics' asceticism.

'Know me, O Son of Pritha, as   10
the eternal seed in all beings,
the mind of the intelligent,
the splendor of the radiant!

'I am the might of the mighty,   11
freed from passion and desire,
I am desire unopposed
to law, O Bull of Bharatas.

'And know that states of being which   12
are pure or passionate or dark,
proceed from me—however, I
am not in them: they are in me!

'By these three states of being, made   13
of the three qualities, this world
is deluded, unaware of
me as higher and eternal.

'Only those who resort to me   14
pass beyond my divine illusion,
formed upon the three qualities
and difficult to penetrate.

'Evildoers, the worst of men,   15
do not find a refuge in me.
With knowledge lost to illusion,
their existence is demonic!

'Arjuna, I am honored by   16
four kinds of benevolent men:
the distressed, the knowledge seeker,
the wealth seeker, and the wise man.

'Of these four, the steadfast wise man,   17
devoted to one, is distinguished,
for I am exceedingly dear
to the wise man, and he to me.

'All these are truly noble, but   18
the wise man I call my own self,
for he of steadfast self abides
in me as his supreme abode.

'After being reborn often,   19
the wise man takes refuge in me:
"Krishna," he thinks, "is all that is!"
Such a great soul is hard to find.

'Those who are bereft of knowledge   20
by these or those lusts turn to gods
of this or that persuasion, being
overruled by their own natures.

'Whoever has the wish to worship   21
whatever god-form faithfully,
it is I who truly grant him
a faith that is immovable.

'Yoked in this faith, the devotee   22
desires to propitiate
that god for answering the prayers
which were granted by me only!

'Fleeting are the results for those   23
who are weak in understanding.
God worshippers go to the gods;
my devotees attain me truly.

'Although I am unmanifest,   24
the foolish think that I have form,
unaware of my eternal,
incomparable higher being.

'Hidden by my magic power,   25
I am not manifest to all;
this foolish world cannot perceive
me as birthless and eternal.

'I know those who have crossed over,   26
Arjuna, and the living too;
I know the beings yet to be,
but I am known by none whatever.

'Deluded by duality   27
arising out of lust and hate,
all beings in creation are
deceived, O Scorcher of the Foe.

'But those whose sins are ended, those   28
whose good deeds have brought them merit,
undeceived by duality,
they worship me with steadfast vows.

'Those who strive for liberation   29
from age and death, relying on me,
know Brahman and know all action,
and know the Self that is supreme.

'And those who know me as Supreme   30
Being and God and Sacrifice,
have steadfast minds and will know me
even at the time of dying.'"

chapter

8

"Arjuna said,

'O Supreme One, what is Brahman? 1
What is the self? What is action?
What undergirds all creation?
What undergirds the Supreme God?

'Who is the Lord of Sacrifice, 2
and how does he live in this flesh?
How are you known by steadfast selves
at end time, O Demon Slayer?'

"The Blessed Lord said,

'Known as the essence of the Self,   3
undying Brahman is supreme.
The power by which all creatures
come to exist is called action.

'Transient being is the physical;   4
and the spirit is the divine.
Here in this flesh I am the Lord
of Sacrifice, O Bharata.

'At the end time, mind fixed on me,   5
one relinquishing his body
goes forth from it to my being,
without a doubt in this instance.

'Whatever state of being one   6
holds in mind, he will attain to,
always changed to that condition
when he leaves his corpse, Arjuna.

'And so, at all times, meditate   7
upon me! Fight, O Warrior!
With mind and intellect fixed on me,
you will attain me, without doubt!

'Steadfast in yogic discipline,   8
thoughts not straying to another,
while meditating, Arjuna,
one goes to the Supreme Person.

'One meditating on the ancient poet,   9
the ruler who is smaller than an atom,
form unimaginable, all-supporting,
the sun-colored one from beyond the darkness,

'drawing the vital breath between his eyebrows,   10
motionless in mind at the time of dying,
yoked by yoga and guided by devotion,
he will approach the divine, Supreme Person.

'What students of the *Vedas* call "the deathless,"   11
which passionless ascetics wish to enter,
and lead chaste lives in order they may do so—
I will explain this path to you now, briefly.

'Having closed all the body's gates,   12
confining mind within the heart,
placing one's own breath in the head,
firm in yogic concentration,

'uttering the Brahmanic oм,   13
and meditating upon me,
who sheds his body and goes forth,
that one attains the highest goal.

'For one of never-straying mind, 14
who constantly remembers me,
for the yogi constantly yoked,
I am quite easily attained.

'Having approached me, the great selves 15
gone to the supreme perfection
are not reborn to this transient
abode of suffering and pain.

'All the way up to Brahma's realm 16
the worlds are reborn, Arjuna,
but those who have resort to me
are not found subject to rebirth.

'Such men know a Brahmanic day 17
which lasts for a thousand ages,
and a night equal in its length;
these truly know the day and night.

'When day arrives, appearances 18
all come from the unmanifest,
dissolving at approach of night,
and are unmanifest once more.

'Repeatedly caused to exist, 19
this vast aggregate of beings
perforce dissolves when night comes on,
returning with returning day.

'Even higher and more ancient   20
is another unmanifest state;
this, when all beings are destroyed
in the destruction, does not die.

'Undying, this unmanifest   21
is said to be the supreme goal
from which there is no returning.
That place is my supreme abode.

'This is the Supreme One, attained   22
by unwavering devotion;
within this all beings abide,
this is what is all-pervading!

'But now, O Bull of Bharatas,   23
I will inform you where in time
those departed yogis go,
those who do, or do not, return.

'Fire, light, day, the moon's bright fortnight,   24
six months of the northern going,
those departing, Brahman-knowing
men go forth then unto Brahman.

'Smoke and night, the moon's dark fortnight,   25
six months of the southern going,
the yogi, with the moon's light glowing,
returns to earth to be reborn.

'There are two paths, the light and dark,   26
both thought to be perpetual;
by one he goes not to return,
but by the other he returns.

'Knowing these two paths, Arjuna,   27
the yogi is not deluded.
Therefore, O Son of Pritha, be
always disciplined by yoga!

'The yogi, having known all this, surpasses   28
merit attained by study of the *Vedas*,
by gifts and sacrifices, self-denial—
the yogi goes to the primal, highest place.'"

chapter

9

"The Blessed Lord said,

'But now I will explain to you,   1
who do not scoff, this deepest secret:
your discerning knowledge of it
will liberate you from evil.

'This secret wisdom of the kings   2
is the greatest purifier,
self-evident and righteous too,
a joy to practice and eternal.

'Men lacking faith in this virtue,   3
Arjuna, not attaining me,
come back again, reborn into
the cycle of transmigration.

'This universe is filled with me,   4
with my unmanifested form;
all beings here abide in me
but I do not abide in them.

'Yet beings do not dwell in me.   5
Behold my majestic power,
creating and sustaining them!
But it does not abide in them.

'As the great wind that stands in space   6
eternally goes everywhere,
so every being everywhere
abides in me. Reflect on this!

'When one age ends, all beings go   7
to my own material nature,
O Son of Kunti; I send them forth
again when the next age begins.

'Resting upon my own nature,   8
I send forth this whole helpless group,
this multitude of beings, by
the very power of my nature.

'Nor do these actions fetter me 9
at all, O Conqueror of Wealth;
indifferent to them, I sit
among them, wholly unattached.

'Nature, with me as overseer, 10
brings forth both still and moving forms;
because of this, the universe
goes round and round, O Son of Kunti.

'Deluded men disesteem me 11
for dwelling in a human form,
all unaware of my higher
nature as Great Lord of Beings.

'Those of fruitless hopes and actions, 12
those of vain and empty knowledge,
abide in a delusional
demonic, devilish nature!

'But the great souls, O Son of Pritha, 13
at rest in my divine nature,
worship me single-mindedly,
known as the deathless source of beings.

'Forever glorifying me, 14
and striving with firm observance,
honoring me with devotion,
the ever steadfast worship me.

'I am worshipped by yet others   15
in the sacrifice of knowledge,
as the one and as the many,
manifold and omniscient.

'I am the rite, the sacrifice,   16
I am the offering, the herb,
I am the mantra and the *ghee*,
I am fire and oblation;

'the father of this universe,   17
its mother and grandfather too;
object of knowledge, soma-strainer,
sacred OM, the three chief *Vedas*;

'I am the way, the Lord, the witness;   18
abode, refuge and companion;
origin, death, and all between;
sepulcher and treasure horde.

'I radiate heat, Arjuna,   19
I hold rain back and let it go,
I am immortal life and death,
I am being and non-being.

'Soma drinkers, well versed in the three *Vedas*,   20
striving for heaven, cleansed by sacrifices,
reaching the pure and longed-for world of Indra,
will feast upon the gods' own sacred pleasures!

'Having enjoyed the spacious world of heaven, 21
merit exhausted, they return to this one;
conforming to the law of the three *Vedas*,
desiring desires, they but come and go here.

'Those men who single-mindedly   22
worship me without wavering,
the steadfast ones, I satisfy
their needs, and what is theirs, protect.

'Even the faithful who worship   23
other gods, O Son of Kunti,
even they also worship me,
though not in accord with custom.

'For I am the Lord and only   24
enjoyer of all sacrifices,
but they do not recognize my
reality, and so they fall.

'To the gods go their worshippers,   25
as to the ancestors go theirs,
and to spirits, theirs; but those who
sacrifice to me, go to me.

'Who with devotion offers me   26
a leaf or flower, water, fruit,
I will taste from that steadfast self,
anything devoutly offered.

'Let anything done or tasted, 27
anything given or endured,
O Son of Kunti, be transformed
into an offering to me!

'Thus freed from the bonds of action, 28
and from its good and evil fruit,
self-disciplined by self-denial,
delivered, you will come to me.

'I am the same in all beings, 29
and dislike none and none hold dear,
but those devout in my worship
are within me and I in them.

'Even the evildoer, if 30
he worships me and no other,
is considered to be righteous,
truly, for his resolution.

'The one whose self is virtuous 31
goes swiftly to eternal peace,
O Son of Kunti. Understand,
no devotee of mine is lost!

'By having found refuge in me, 32
even those out of evil wombs,
such as women, merchants, servants,
go to the supreme goal as well.

'How much more so may the Brahmins   33
and the devoted royal seers!
Finding yourself in this transient
world of misfortune, worship me!

'Be fixed on me in devotion,   34
sacrificing, doing reverence!
So steadied, you will come to me,
having me as your supreme aim!'"

chapter

10

"The Blessed Lord said,

'Once more, O Mighty Warrior,   1
hear from my lips my matchless word,
which I address to you, Beloved,
from my care for your well-being!

'Neither the multitude of gods   2
nor great seers know my origin,
for I am the true source of all
gods and great seers in any case.

'Who knows me as the world's Great Lord,   3
birthless and without beginning,
is undeluded among men
and liberated from all ills.

'Intelligence, knowledge, clarity,   4
forbearance, truth and self-restraint,
tranquility, joy and sorrow,
being, non-being, fear and courage;

'non-violence, equanimity,   5
austerity, contentedness,
gifts, honor, shame; the diverse states
of being spring from me only.

'In the past the seven great seers   6
and the four law-giving Manus,
progenitors of humankind,
originated in my mind.

'Who truly knows this manifest   7
power and mastery of mine
is joined to me, without a doubt,
by the unwavering yoga.

'I am the origin of all,   8
and from me everything proceeds;
and thinking so, the learned ones,
filled with my being, worship me.

'Mind fixed on me, breath gone to me,   9
enlightening one another
and speaking of me constantly,
they are content and they rejoice.

'To those who are yoked constantly,   10
and are joyful in their worship,
I give the yoga of higher mind,
by which they will attain to me.

'So, from my compassion for them,   11
I who dwell in their own beings
destroy ignorance-born darkness
with the shining lamp of knowledge.'

   "Arjuna said,

'You are the consummate Brahman,   12
matchless abode and purifier,
the eternal sacred person,
god unborn and all-pervading.

'So all the wise men say of you,   13
and the divine seer Narada,
and Asita, Devala too,
and Vyasa, and you yourself.

'I think all this to be the truth   14
you tell me, O Handsome-Haired One,
for neither gods nor demons know
your manifestations, O Lord.

'Through yourself only, do you know   15
your own self, O Highest Person,
Creator God, Lord of Beings,
God of Gods, Lord of the Universe!

'Please describe for me completely   16
your divine manifestations
by which, having permeated
these worlds, you abide in them.

'How may I know you, O Yogin,   17
reflecting on you constantly?
In what diverse states of being
are you to be imagined, Lord?

'Once more explain in great detail   18
your power and your diverse forms,
for I cannot hear enough of
the deathless nectar of your speech!'

"The Blessed Lord said,

'Hear! I will tell you of my own   19
divine self-manifestations,
my main ones, O Best of Kurus,
for my extension has no end.

'I am the Self, situated   20
in the heart of every being,
for whom I am the origin,
midpoint and end, O Thick-Haired One.

'Of the Adityas I am Vishnu,   21
of lights I am the radiant sun,
of storm gods I am Marici,
and of the stars I am the moon.

'Of *Vedas*, the *Sama Veda*;   22
of the gods I am Vasava;
of the senses I am the mind;
of beings I am consciousness.

'Of the Rudras I am Shiva,   23
of Rakshasas, Kubera,
of the Vasus I am Agni,
of the mountains I am Meru.

'Know, O Son of Pritha, I   24
am the chief of household priests;
of generals I am Skanda;
of the waters I am Ocean.

'Of the great seers I am Bhrigu,   25
I am the OM of utterances,
of sacrifice, the muttered prayer,
of mountains, the Himalayas.

'Of trees I am the sacred fig,   26
of the divine seers, Narada,
of Gandharvas, Citraratha,
of the perfected, Kapila.

'Of horses, the one Indra rides,   27
born of nectar; of elephants,
Indra's lordly Airavata;
of mortal men I am the king.

'Of weapons I am the thunderbolt,   28
of cows, the wish-fulfilling cow;
I am Kandarpa, god of love;
of serpents I am Vasuki.

'Of Naga-snakes I am Ananta,   29
of water-creatures I am Varuna,
of ancestors I am Aryaman,
of punishers I am Yama.

'Of demons I am Prahlada,   30
of regulators I am Time,
of animals I am the lion,
and of the birds, Vainateya.

'Of purifiers I am wind,   31
of weapon bearers I am Rama,
Makara of the sea monsters,
And of rivers I am Ganges.

'Of creations I am beginning,   32
middle and the end, Arjuna;
of sciences, that of the Self,
of speakers I am the discourse.

'Of letters I am the letter "A,"   33
of compound words the conjunctive;
I am indeed undying time,
and the omniscient arranger.

'I am death, the all-destroying,   34
and the source of what will happen;
of feminine things, fame, wealth, speech,
memory, wisdom, courage, patience.

'Of Saman-chants, Bhradsama,   35
of meters I am Gayatri,
of months I am the very first,
of seasons, flower-bearing spring.

'I am the gambling of cheats,   36
I am the brilliance of the bright,
I am victory and effort,
the virtue of the virtuous.

'Of the Vrishnis I am Krishna,   37
of Pandavas I am Arjuna,
and of the sages, Vyasa,
of poets I am Ushana.

'I am the clout of the rulers,   38
the advice of those who wish to win;
of secrets I am the silence,
and the knowledge of those who know.

'And I am that which is the seed   39
within all beings, Arjuna;
without me, nothing can exist,
whether moving or motionless.

'Endless, my manifestations,   40
O Scorcher of the Enemy.
But these have been declared by me
as explanations of my force.

'Know that the origin of any 41
being, however glorious
or powerful, is never more
than a fraction of my brilliance!

'But Arjuna, what purpose does 42
all this extensive knowledge serve?
With but one fragment of myself
I constantly support this world.' "

chapter

11

"Arjuna said,

'As a result of your kindness   1
in speaking of that greatest secret
recognized as the Supreme Self,
I have been left undeluded.

'I have, in detail, heard you speak   2
Of creatures' origins and ends,
and of your eternal greatness,
O One of Lotus-Petal-Eyes.

'This is just as you have spoken 3
about yourself, O Supreme Lord.
I desire to behold your
lordly form, O Supreme Spirit.

'If you think it is possible 4
for me to see this, then, O God,
O Lord of Yoga, allow me
to behold your eternal Self!'

"The Blessed Lord said,

'O Son of Pritha, look upon 5
my hundredfold, no, thousandfold
forms various and celestial,
forms of diverse shapes and colors!

'Behold the Adityas and Vasus, 6
the Rudras, Ashvins and Maruts,
many unseen previously!
Behold these wonders, Arjuna!

'Here behold all the universe, 7
beings moving and motionless,
standing as one in my body,
and all else that you wish to see!

'Because you are unable to   8
behold me with your mortal eye,
I give you one that is divine:
Behold my majestic power!'

Sanjaya said,

"And after saying this, O King,   9
Vishnu, the great Lord of Yoga,
revealed his supreme, majestic
form to him, the Son of Pritha.

"That form has many eyes and mouths,   10
and many wonders visible,
with many sacred ornaments,
and many sacred weapons raised.

"Clothed in sacred wreaths and garments,   11
with many sacred fragrances,
and comprising every wonder,
the infinite, omniscient god!

"If in the sky a thousand suns   12
should have risen all together,
the brilliance of it would be like
the brilliance of that Great-Souled One.

"And then the Son of Pandu saw   13
the universe standing as one,
divided up in diverse ways,
embodied in the god of gods.

"Then Arjuna, seized by wonder,   14
with his hair standing up on end,
with joined hands raised to his bowed head
in reverential gesture, said,

'I see all gods, O God, within your body,   15
and every kind of being all collected,
and the Lord Brahma seated on his lotus,
with all the seers and with the sacred serpents.

'I see your many arms, your bellies, faces;   16
I see you everywhere, whose form is boundless,
endless, with no beginning and no middle,
Lord of the Universe, whose form your own is.

'I see you crowned and armed with mace
     and discus,   17
a splendid mass of many-sided brilliance
almost impossible to grasp completely,
limitless blazing of the sun and fire!

'You, the unchanging object of all knowledge,   18
you, the ultimate refuge of this cosmos,
you, the eternal law's immortal champion,
and, as I now believe, primeval spirit!

'Infinite power, unbegun, unending;   19
arms without number, sun and moon for vision;
I see your fire-blazing mouth devour
whole worlds entire, scorched by your own brilliance!

'All between earth and heaven is pervaded   20
only by you, in every direction;
seeing your wondrous, terrible appearance,
Almighty Soul, the three worlds quake and shudder!

'Throngs of gods enter you; some, fearful,
     praise you,   21
and having greeted you with reverent gestures,
perfected ones and sages in assembly
celebrate you with praises in abundance!

'Rudras, Adityas, Vasus, Saddhyas, All-Gods,   22
Storm Gods, the Asvins, steam-inhaling forebears,
Gandharvas, Yakshas, demon Asuras,
and the Perfected, all behold you awestruck!

'Seeing your form so mighty in appearance,   23
so many mouths and eyes, thighs, feet and bellies,
and with those fangs of yours that are so dreadful,
all the worlds tremble, terrified as I am!

'With gaping mouths and eyes gigantic blazing,   24
you touch the sky and burn with many colors!
So I have seen you, and my spirit shuddered,
calmness and courage lost to me, O Vishnu!

'So terrifying your mouths in appearance,   25
resembling the fires of destruction,
disoriented, I can find no refuge,
O Lord of Gods, O World Abode, have mercy!

'Into you pour the sons of Dhritarashtra   26
with all the earthly rulers there assembled,
Bhisma and Drona too, along with Karna,
and with them also our leading warriors!

'Quickly they spill into your mouths so fearsome, 27
your jaws that all with fangs are thickly studded,
some men with heads grotesquely crushed and mangled,
between your teeth in desperation clinging!

'Just as the many torrents of the rivers   28
flow ever onward into the great ocean,
so do the heroes of this world of mortals
enter your flaming mouths seen in the distance.

'Like moths that hasten onward till they enter   29
the blazing flame in which they find destruction,
just so the worlds, in hastening to enter
your gaping mouths, all seek out their destruction.

'With every mouth ablaze, you lick with flaming   30
tongues the worlds which on every side you swallow,
and fill the cosmos wholly with your brilliance,
your awful light that blazes forth, O Vishnu!

'Who are you? Tell me, Lord of Dread
   Appearance!   31
Homage to you! O Best of Gods, have mercy!
For I would understand you, Primal Being,
whose purpose is beyond my comprehension!'

"The Blessed Lord said,

'I am almighty time, the world-destroying,   32
and to destroy these worlds I have arisen!
Those warriors arrayed in lines opposing
your men, even without you, will have perished!

'Arise, therefore, and seize upon your glory!   33
With your foe conquered, enjoy thriving kingship!
I have destroyed your enemy already:
serve as my tool, O Ambidextrous Archer!

'Kill! Do not hesitate to take on Drona,   34
Bhishma, Jayadratha, Karna, and the others,
warrior-heroes I have caused to perish!
You will destroy your enemies in battle!'

    Sanjaya said,

"With his joined hands pressed in reverential
    gesture   35
to his bowed head, Arjuna, struck with terror
at hearing the words of the Handsome-Haired One,
humbly bowed down and stammered out to Krishna:

"Arjuna said,

'By your renown, the universe rejoices   36
and takes its pleasure, O Bristling-Haired One!
Terrified demons scatter, the assembly
of the perfected ones all bows before you!

'Why should they not, O Great Soul, even
        greater   37
than Brahma? You, the primary creator,
infinite Lord of Gods, home of the cosmos,
deathless beyond both being and non-being.

'You are the primal god, the ancient person,   38
you are this universe's highest refuge:
knower and known, and the supreme condition!
Infinite form suffusing all the cosmos!

'You are the moon, Vayu, Yama, Varuna;   39
the Lord of Creatures and the Great-Grandfather.
May there be a thousand times made reverence,
reverence to you, and again, reverence!

'May you be greeted everywhere with bowing,   40
before, behind you, everywhere obeisance!
You are unmeasured strength, infinite power,
and you are all by being all-pervasive!

'If I have thought of you as friend and spoken   41
impetuously, "Hey, friend, Yadava, Krishna—"
in ignorance of your majestic power,
out of confusion, even with affection,

'If ever with disrespect I treated you,   42
made sport of you while resting, seated, dining,
O Unshaken One, alone or with others,
I ask you, measureless one, for your pardon!

Father of all the world, the still and moving,   43
you are what it worships and its teacher;
with none your match, how could there be one greater
in the three worlds, O Power-Without-Equal?

'Making obeisance, lying in prostration,   44
I beg your indulgence, praiseworthy ruler;
as father to son, as one friend to another,
as lover to beloved, show your mercy!

'I am pleased to have seen what never has been   45
seen before, yet my mind quakes in its terror:
show me, O God, your human form; have mercy,
O Lord of Gods, abode of all the cosmos!

'I wish to see you even as I did once,   46
wearing a diadem, with mace and discus;
assume that form now wherein you have four arms,
O thousand-armed, of every form the master!'

"The Blessed Lord said,

'For you, Arjuna, by my grace and favor,   47
this highest form is brought forth by my power,
of splendor made, universal, endless, primal,
and never seen before by any other.

'Not Vedic sacrifice nor recitation,   48
gifts, rituals, strenuous austerities,
will let this form of mine be seen by any
mortal but you, O Hero of the Kurus!

'You should not tremble, nor dwell in confusion   49
at seeing such a terrible appearance.
With your fears banished and your mind now cheerful,
look once again upon my form, Arjuna.'

    Sanjaya said,

"So Krishna, having spoken to Arjuna,   50
stood before him once more in his own aspect;
having resumed again a gentle body,
the Great Soul calmed the one who had been
    frightened.

"Arjuna said,

'Seeing once again your gentle,   51
human form now, I am composed,
O Agitator of Mankind;
my mind is restored to normal.'

"The Blessed Lord said,

'It is difficult to see this   52
aspect of me that you have seen;
even the gods are forever
desirous of seeing it.

'Not by studying the *Vedas*,   53
nor even by austerities,
and not by gifts or sacrifice,
may I be seen as you saw me;

'but by devotion undisturbed   54
can I be truly seen and known,
and entered into, Arjuna,
O Scorcher of the Enemy!

'Who acts for me, depends on me,   55
devoutly, without attachment
or hatred for another being,
comes to me, O Son of Pandu!'"

chapter

12

"Arjuna said,

'Who are more knowing of yoga,   1
those who worship you steadfastly,
or those other ones who worship
the eternal unseen Brahman?'

"The Blessed Lord said,

'Those who, steadfast in their yoga,   2
worship me with attentive minds,
endowed with the most perfect faith,
are considered the more knowing.

'Those who worship the unchanging,   3
unseen and inexplicable,
the omnipresent beyond thought,
the summit-dwelling constancy;

'who restrain their many senses,   4
who practice equanimity,
rejoicing in the welfare of
all creatures, also come to me.

'A greater toil is known by those   5
whose minds cleave to the unseen Brahman;
embodied ones attain that goal
only with much more exertion.

'But those who yield all acts to me,   6
intent on me as the highest,
and worship me, meditating
with undistracted discipline;

'O Son of Pritha, presently   7
I will redeem, from the ocean
of death and transmigration, those
whose conscious minds have entered me.

'But fix your mind on me alone,   8
and place your intellect in me:
I will be your only abode
from that time forth, without a doubt!

'Or if you are unable to   9
keep your mind fixed on me always,
then by the practice of yoga
seek to attain me, Arjuna!

'If incapable of practice,   10
be intent upon my action,
and just by acting for my sake
you will attain to perfection.

'And if incapable of that,   11
lean upon my yogic power;
abandon all the fruits of
action, and act with self restraint!

'Value knowledge over practice,   12
meditation over knowledge;
highest is renunciation,
whence comes, immediately, peace.

'Who does not hate any being,   13
is friendly and compassionate,
without possessiveness and ego,
the same in grief and joy, enduring,

'the yogi who lives in content,   14
firmly resolved and self-restrained,
whose higher mind is fixed on me,
who is devout is dear to me.

'One from whom the world does not shrink,   15
one who does not shrink from the world,
freed from distress, from impatience,
from fear and joy, is dear to me.

'Who sits apart, indifferent,   16
pure, able, free of anxiety;
who has abandoned all busyness,
and is devout, is dear to me.

'Who neither hates nor rejoices,   17
who neither grieves nor desires,
abjuring pleasant and unpleasant,
and is devout, is dear to me.

'He who is one with foe and friend,   18
and one in honor and disgrace,
in cold and heat, joy and anguish,
freed from attachment to results,

'with one response to praise or blame,   19
contented with whatever comes,
silent, homeless, steady in mind,
devout, he is most dear to me!

'Those who honor this immortal   20
law, as I have described above,
keeping their faith, intent on me
as highest, are most dear to me!'"

chapter

13

"Arjuna said,

'O Handsome-Haired One, I would know
of nature and of the spirit,
of the field and of its knower,
of knowledge and of its object.'

"The Blessed Lord said,

'This body, O Son of Kunti,   I
is that which is known as the field;
one who knows it is said to be
the field's knower, by those who know.

'Know me as knower of the field   2
in every field, O Bharata!
I regard knowledge of the field
and its knower as true knowledge.

'What this field is, what it is like,   3
of its changes, from whence they come,
of its knower and his power,
hear me speak of them concisely!

'It has often been sung by seers   4
in Vedic hymns of many kinds,
with lines sacred to the Brahmins
unarguably reasoned out.

'The great elements, the ego,   5
the higher mind, the unmanifest,
and the eleven faculties
with the five fields of sense-action;

'desire, hatred, pleasure, pain,   6
the body, consciousness, resolve;
all these, in brief, compose the field
with its capacity for change.

'Humility, sincerity,   7
non-violence, patience, candor,
docility, integrity,
stability and self-restraint;

'firm detachment from sense-objects,   8
egoism wholly absent,
mindfulness of the faults of birth,
death, old age, disease and anguish;

'non-attachment, with no clinging   9
to son, wife, home, *et cetera*,
and constant equanimity
in what is longed for or avoided;

'and with no other discipline,   10
unwavering in love of me,
frequenting secluded places
and avoiding crowds of people;

'seeking the knowledge of the Self,   11
seeing into reality:
this is declared to be knowledge.
What is not this is ignorance.

'I shall address the to-be-known,   12
by which one becomes immortal;
the birthless, matchless Brahman, said
neither to be nor to be not.

'Its hand and foot are everywhere,   13
and everywhere its eye, head, face;
its ears on earth are everywhere;
it abides, all-enveloping.

'Apprehended by the senses   14
and yet detached and free from them,
all-maintaining, unattached to
the qualities that it enjoys.

'Within all beings and without,   15
moving and motionless at once
in uncomprehended fineness,
it dwells afar and yet nearby.

'Undistributed in beings,   16
and yet existing as though shared,
to be known as the sustainer,
all-destroying, all-creating.

'This is also called the light   17
of lights that lie beyond darkness;
knowledge, its object and its goal,
located in the hearts of all.

'The field, knowledge, and its object,   18
here have been considered briefly.
In grasping this, my devotee
arrives at my state of being.

'Know that matter and spirit are   19
both of them without beginning!
Know as well what transformations
and qualities spring from matter!

'Matter is said to be the reason   20
for agency, cause and effect.
Spirit has been called the reason
for apprehending joy and sorrow.

'The spirit that dwells in matter   21
knows qualities born of matter.
Attachment to these qualities
leads to birth in good and bad wombs.

'The highest spirit in this body   22
is called witness and consenter,
supporter, experiencer,
the Great Lord and the Highest Self.

'One who therefore knows both spirit   23
and matter with its qualities,
existing in whatever way,
will not be subject to rebirth.

'Some see the Self within the Self   24
by the Self through meditation,
others by Samkhya yoga,
or the discipline of action.

'Yet some who do not know of this,   25
worship what they hear from others;
they also travel beyond death,
devoted to what they have heard.

'Know, O Bharata, that any 26
being, whether still or moving,
is born out of the union of
the field and knower of the field!

'Who sees the Supreme Lord existing 27
equally in all beings
and not perishing when they do,
truly sees, O Son of Kunti!

'Indeed, when he beholds the Lord 28
existing equally everywhere,
he does not injure Self by self
and so goes to the highest goal.

'And he who sees that actions are 29
entirely performed by matter,
the Self having no agency,
that one truly sees, Arjuna.

'When one observes diverse states of 30
being abiding in the one,
diverging only from that one,
then he attains the absolute.

'Though located in the body, 31
this everlasting supreme Self
without a source or qualities,
does not act and is not defiled.

'Like the all-pervading ether,   32
so subtle it cannot be stained,
so the Self, situated in
the body, cannot be defiled.

'Just as the one sun illumines   33
this world entire by itself,
so the field's owner shines upon
the entire field, O Bharata!

'Those who with the eye of knowledge   34
distinguish between field and knower
and understand deliverance
from nature's bonds, attain Brahman.'"

chapter

14

"The Blessed Lord said,

'And furthermore, I shall declare   1
the highest knowledge and the best;
having known this, all the sages
are gone hence to supreme perfection.

'Resorting to this knowledge, they   2
attain to my identity;
not born even at creation,
they hold fast at dissolution.

'My womb is the great absolute,   3
in which I place the embryo;
the origin of all beings
is in that source, O Bharata.

'Whatever forms that arise in   4
other wombs, O Son of Kunti,
have *their* womb in the absolute;
I am the seed-sowing father.

'Purity, passion and darkness,   5
the qualities born of nature,
bind the imperishable one
fast in the body, Arjuna.

'There, immaculate purity,   6
brightly shining, undiseased,
binds by attachments both to joy
and to knowledge, O Sinless One.

'Learn that passion's disposition   7
arises from thirst attachment,
and fetters the embodied one
by the attachment to action!

'Learn that ignorance-born darkness   8
confuses all embodied ones,
and binds by sleep, by laziness,
and negligence, O Bharata!

'Purity brings about attachment   9
to happiness; passion, to action;
knowledge-hiding darkness brings a-
bout attachment to negligence.

'Passion and darkness overcome,   10
purity comes into being,
as do passion and darkness, when
each overcomes the other two.

'When the light of knowledge shines   11
through all the body's apertures,
then it ought to be apparent
that purity is dominant.

'Greed, activity, busyness,   12
desire and disquietude
are born when passion dominates,
O Bull of the Bharatas.

'The absence of enlightenment,   13
indolence, negligence, delusion—
all these come into being when
darkness prevails, O Joy of Kuru.

'But when an embodied one dies   14
while purity is dominant,
that one attains the stainless worlds
of those knowing of the highest.

'Who dies when passion dominates   15
is born with those attached to action;
likewise, one who dies in darkness
is born to a deluded womb.

'The fruit of action well performed   16
is said to be immaculate,
but misery is passion's fruit,
and that of darkness, ignorance.

'Knowledge is born from purity,   17
and avarice comes from passion;
distraction and delusion come
from darkness, as does ignorance.

Those firm in purity ascend;   18
the passionate stay in the middle;
those governed by the lowest mode,
the mode of darkness, go below.

'When the seer sees no other   19
agent besides the qualities,
and knows that which is above them,
he attains my state of being.

'Transcending these three qualities,   20
the body's source, an embodied one
becomes immortal when released
from birth, death, old age and anguish.'

"Arjuna said,

'One transcending these qualities,   21
by what signs is he known, O Lord?
How does that one conduct himself?
How are the qualities transcended?'

"The Blessed Lord said,

'When they occur, he does not hate   22
splendor, activity, delusion,
O Pandava; nor does that one
desire them not to occur.

'One seated as if indifferent,   23
undisturbed by the qualities,
who thinks, "The qualities exist,"
and stands firm and unwavering,

'indifferent to pain and joy,   24
not preferring gold to glebe,
the same with cherished as despised,
the same whether praised or censured,

'the same in honor or dishonor,   25
not taking sides with friend or foe,
who gives up all undertakings,
is said to transcend the qualities.

'And who unswervingly serves me   26
with the practice of devotion,
transcending these three qualities,
is fit to be one with Brahman.

'For I am the support of Brahman,   27
and of the imperishable,
and of the everlasting law,
and of the one and only bliss.'"

chapter

15

"The Blessed Lord said,

'They speak of an eternal fig tree   1
with root above and branch below,
of which the leaves are Vedic chants;
he who knows this knows the *Vedas*.

'Fed by the qualities, its branches spread out   2
above and below, its shoots are sense-objects,
with roots stretched out extensively beneath it,
which, in the world of men, give rise to action.

'Here in the world, its form is imperceptible,   3
neither its end, duration, nor beginning;
with the firm ax of non-attachment, having
chopped down this holy, strong-rooted fig tree,

'only then is that place to be sought after   4
from which none may return of those who reach it,
"And I take refuge in that primal person
whence, long ago, activity once issued."

'Humbly, having vanquished faults of attachment,   5
spurning desire, in the Supreme Self always,
freed from dualities of pain and pleasure,
to that changeless realm come the undeluded.

'Neither the sun nor moon nor fire   6
illuminates that place from whence
none return once they have gone there.
That place is my supreme abode.

'In this world the merest fragment   7
of me becomes eternal soul,
draws to itself mind and the five
senses that abide in nature.

'When the Lord assumes a body   8
and when he steps away from it,
departing, he takes these with him,
as wind wafts odors from their source.

'Presiding over hearing, sight,   9
touch, taste and smell, along with mind,
the embodied Self takes pleasure
in the senses and their objects.

'In his presence or departure   10
or pleasured by the qualities,
the deluded do not see him:
those with the eye of knowledge do.

'Striving, the yogins see the Lord   11
situated within the Self;
unthinking, unperfected selves,
although striving, do not see him.

'The splendor that the sun gives off,   12
illuming all the universe,
found in the moon and found in fire—
Know that this splendor is my own!

'Diffused through earth, by energy   13
I sustain all living creatures;
as juicy soma, Lord of Plants,
I make all the verdure flourish.

'Now become digestive fire   14
dwelling in all breathing bodies,
conjoined to breathing in and out,
I break down the four kinds of food.

'And into everyone's heart I am entered;   15
from me come memory, knowledge, and reason;
I am the only subject of the *Vedas*,
Vedanta's maker, knower of the Veda.

'This world knows two kinds of being: 16
those who perish, those who do not;
all creatures die, save for the unchanging one, called the eternal.

'But the highest person is another,   17
known as the Supreme Being,
who, having entered the three worlds,
bears them as their eternal Lord.

'Being beyond the perishable   18
and higher than imperishable,
in this world and in the *Vedas*
I am called the Supreme Person.

'Therefore, he who, undeluded,   19
knows me as the Supreme Person,
he, all-knowing, shares in me with
all his being, Arjuna.

'Thus is this most secret doctrine   20
proclaimed by me, O Blameless One;
one who awakens to this knows
wisdom and fulfills all duty.'"

chapter 16

"The Blessed Lord said,

'Fearlessness, purity of heart,   1
dwelling in the yoga of knowledge,
giving, self-restraint, sacrifice,
recitation, penance, straightness;

'non-violence, truth and calmness,   2
renunciation, slander-shunning,
compassion, freedom from all lusts,
gentleness, modesty, steadiness;

'Vigor, patience, courage, cleanliness,   3
absence of malice and of pride;
these qualities endow those born
to a divine fate, Arjuna.

'Hypocrisy, arrogance, pride,   4
anger, a harsh way of speaking
and ignorance endow one born
to a demonic destiny.

'The divine state leads to freedom,   5
the demonic into bondage.
You have been born to the former,
so do not grieve, O Pandava!

'In this world are two kinds of beings,   6
the divine and the demonic;
I have described the first at length,
now learn from me of the latter.

'Demonic men are unaware   7
of when to act and when to cease.
Truth, purity, and good behavior
are not to be found in such men.

'"The universe," they say, "is false,   8
is baseless and without a God,
not produced one by the other."
How else, then? "Brought about by lust!"

'Holding this view, men of lost selves,   9
men of little intelligence
and cruel deeds, rise up, become
foes out to destroy the cosmos.

Subject to insatiable lusts,   10
full of hypocrisy and pride,
intoxicated on delusions,
their observances are impure.

'Clinging to immeasurable   11
anxiety, whose end is death,
holding pleasure their highest aim,
they are certain that this is all.

'Bound by a hundred snares of hope,   12
devoted to lusts and anger,
unjustly they seek piles of wealth
to gratify their desires.

'"Today I have acquired *this*,   13
that, I will obtain tomorrow;
these now belong to me and soon
those riches will become my own!

'"That foe is dead by my doing   14
and I shall slay even others;
I am the Lord, the Enjoyer,
accomplished, mighty, and content!

'"I am wealthy, of noble birth,   15
what other man is my equal?
I will sacrifice, give and rejoice,"
they say, deceived by ignorance.

'Borne off by their imaginings,   16
ensnared by the web of folly,
attached to gratification,
they fall into an impure hell.

'Self-centered and refractory,   17
intoxicated by their wealth,
they sacrifice in name only,
falsely, not as they are bidden.

'Attached to ego, force and pride,   18
as well as to lust and anger,
these malcontented men hate me
in their own bodies and in others'.

'I forever fling those vile,   19
hate-filled, cruel, impure men
into the cycles of rebirth,
just so, into demonic wombs.

'Not gaining me, the deluded,   20
having entered wombs of demons,
descend from there, birth after birth,
to the lowest place, Arjuna.

'Desire, anger, greediness   21
comprise the threefold gate of hell
truly destructive of the self,
so one should renounce this triad.

'O Son of Kunti, one released   22
from these three doors of the darkness,
proceeds then to the highest place,
O Descendant of Bharata.

'One who, ignoring the commands   23
of scripture, follows his own desires,
does not attain to perfection
nor happiness, nor the highest place.

'Scripture is your authority   24
for what to do and not to do.
Understanding its injunctions,
you are obliged to action here!'"

chapter

17

"Arjuna said,

'What is the status of those who   1
have cast aside the Vedic rules,
but sacrifice in faith, O Krishna?
—The pure, the passionate, the dark?'

"The Blessed Lord said,

'The faith of the embodied ones   2
is of three kinds. Born of itself,
of its own being, it is pure
and passionate and dark. Hear more!

'In every case, faith corresponds   3
to one's own essential nature.
Man is made of faith, Arjuna,
and *is* the very faith he *has*.

'The pure give worship to the gods,   4
the passionate worship demons,
and men of darkness sacrifice
to ghosts and hordes of ancient shades.

'Who suffer dread austerities   5
that are not ordained by scripture,
these ostentatious egotists
endowed with force, lust and passion,

'by whom the body's aggregate   6
of elements suffers tortures,
and I too, within the body—
know them fixed on the demonic!

'Each of the three kinds has its own   7
preference with regard to food,
worship, austerities and gifts;
now hear what distinguishes them!

'Foods dear to the pure-of-being   8
enhance life, virtue, strength and health,
happiness and satisfaction,
are tasty, smooth, firm and pleasant.

'Foods cherished by the passionate 9
are pungent, sour, salty, hot,
sharp, dry and spiced excessively,
causing pain, sorrow and sickness.

'Spoiled and stale and without flavor, 10
putrid and crusted leftovers
unfit for sacrifice are foods
agreeable to the dark-natured.

'Pure sacrifice is offered by 11
those unattached to its results
whose minds are fixed upon the thought
that "This is to be sacrificed."

'That sacrifice which is offered 12
in expectation of results
and showily, O Bharata,
is to be known as passionate!

'Sacrifice without injunction, 13
or food offered, or a mantra,
without gifts given to the priest,
devoid of faith, is seen as darkness.

'Revering the gods, the twice-born; 14
teachers and sages; purity,
truth, chastity, and non-violence:
asceticism of the body.

'Speech not causing agitation,   15
truthful, pleasing, beneficent,
with daily Vedic recitation:
asceticism made of speech.

'Clarity and benevolence,   16
silence along with self-control,
joined with purity-of-being:
asceticism of the mind.

'This three-fold asceticism,   17
faithfully practiced by men yoked
in discipline, without regard
to fruit of action, is called pure.

'Fraudulent asceticism,   18
to gain honor or win favors,
I declare to be passionate,
unsteady and impermanent.

'Austerities involving torture,   19
with a deluded grasp of self,
intended to destroy another,
that is dark asceticism.

'A gift given for its own sake,   20
not in response to prior favors,
worthy the place, time and person,
that gift is known as pure-natured.

'But that gift given with the aim   2 1
of recompense for another,
or one given unwillingly,
that gift is known as passionate.

'The gift given at the wrong place   2 2
and wrong time to one unworthy,
without respect or with contempt
is said to be dark in nature.

'"OM THAT [IS] TRUTH" is said to be   2 3
the symbol of threefold Brahman;
by this were priesthood, *Vedas*, forms
of worship anciently ordained.

'Thus worship, gifts, austerities   2 4
commence after "OM" is uttered,
as provided in the scriptures
by philosophers of Brahman.

'Uttering "TRUTH," without aiming   2 5
at results, those who seek release
offer donations and perform
ascetic acts and sacrifices.

'"TRUTH" designates reality   2 6
and designates goodness also;
O Son of Pritha, the word "TRUTH"
is used for a praiseworthy act.

'In worship, gifts, austerities,   27
"TRUTH" is considered steadfastness,
and any related action
is also designated "TRUTH."

'Oblations or austerities   28
done without faith are called "UNTRUE,"
and have no meaning, Arjuna,
here in this world or hereafter.'"

chapter

✦ 18 ✦

"Arjuna said,

'O Mighty-Armed One, I would know   1
how renunciation differs
from abandonment, O Krishna,
with each considered in its turn.'

"The Blessed Lord said,

'For the seers, renunciation   2
means ceasing to act from desires;
for the clear-eyed, abandonment
is giving up all fruits of action.

'Some wise men say that *all* action   3
is wrong and should be given up;
others exempt sacrificial acts,
gift-giving and austerities.

'Hear my judgment in the matter   4
of abandonment, O Bharata!
For that subject, O Tiger of Men,
has a threefold designation.

'Sacrifice, gifts, austerities   5
should be performed, not abandoned;
sacrifice, donations, hardships
are purifiers of the wise.

'These actions, though, should be performed   6
without attachment to their fruits.
O Son of Pritha, this is my
supreme conviction, without doubt.

'Renunciation of prescribed   7
action is inappropriate;
abandoning it from delusion
is said to be suffused in darkness.

'Who would abandon difficult   8
action from fear of physical pain
does passionate abandonment;
truly he will find it fruitless.

'When acts are performed, Arjuna,　　9
solely out of obligation,
with no attachment to their fruits,
such abandonment is called pure.

'The lightness-filled abandoner,　　10
a wise man cut free from all doubt,
does not hate unpleasant actions,
nor does he cling to pleasant ones.

'Embodied beings are unable　　11
to abandon action wholly;
but one who abandons the fruits
is known as an "abandoner."

'Those who die without renouncing　　12
know the threefold fruit of action:
desired, undesired, mixed.
But for renouncers, there is none.

'O Mighty-Armed One, awaken　　13
to these five causes, taught by me,
declared in the Samkhya doctrine
for the fulfillment of all actions!

'There is the body and the agent,　　14
and instruments of diverse kinds,
and various activities,
and lastly there is providence.

'Whatever action anyone   15
begins by body, speech, or mind,
either proper or improper,
these five causes will be present.

'This being so, who sees himself   16
as the sole doer, does not see,
that incorrectly thinking man
whose intellect is unfinished!

'Who is not egotistical,   17
whose intellect is untainted,
even having slain these people,
he neither slays, nor is he bound.

'Knowledge, the known, and the knower   18
are the threefold prompts to action;
the means, the act, and the agent
are action's threefold components.

'Knowledge, action, and the agent   19
are of three distinct qualities,
as Samkhya doctrine declares;
duly hear about these also!

'Knowledge by which the undying   20
oneness is seen in all beings,
undivided in divisions—
know it as pure in quality!

'Knowledge that sees in all beings   21
their various existences
and sees them all as separate—
know this knowledge as passionate!

'Knowledge attached to one effect   22
as though to all; unreasoning,
slight and without significance—
that knowledge is said to be dark.

'Action restrained and unattached,   23
performed without hate or passion,
without desire for the fruits—
that action is said to be pure.

'That action performed to obtain   24
a desire or done selfishly,
or one performed with great effort,
is declared to be passionate.

'Action undertaken due   25
to delusion, disregarding
strength, injury, death, consequence,
is said to be dark in nature.

'One who is free from attachment,   26
firmly resolved, self-effacing,
unmoved by success or failure,
is said to be a pure agent.

'One who desires fruit of action,   27
greedy, violent, and unchaste,
accompanied by joy and grief,
is called a passionate agent.

'One unrefined, undisciplined,   28
stubborn, false, dishonest, lazy,
depressed and procrastinating,
is called an agent of darkness.

'Now hear the threefold distinction   29
of intellect and resolution
proclaimed completely, each in turn,
according to the qualities.

'Mind that knows action from inaction,   30
right from wrongdoing, fear from courage,
liberation from enslavement
is pure mind, O Son of Pritha.

'Mind that wrongly discriminates   31
between virtue and non-virtue,
the to-be-done and not-to be,
is passionate, O Son of Pritha.

'Mind that, enveloped in its own   32
darkness, considers wrong as right,
and sees all aims as perverted,
O Son of Pritha, is dark mind.

'The firmness that controls the mind,   33
breath, and senses with unswerving
practice of yoga—that firmness is
considered light, O Son of Pritha.

'But firmness by which one maintains   34
virtue, pleasure, and great riches
while longing for the fruits of action
is impassioned, O Son of Pritha.

'Firmness by which the dull-witted   35
do not abandon sleep, fear, grief,
depression, and conceit, is dark
firmness indeed, O Son of Pritha.

'Now learn from me of the threefold   36
joy experienced from practice,
and where one goes to end anguish,
O Bull of the Bharatas!

'That which first resembles poison,   37
but seems like nectar when transformed,
is known as pure happiness, born
out of one's own tranquil spirit.

'That which first resembles nectar   38
due to object-sense connection,
but is like poison when transformed,
is called passionate happiness.

'That happiness which, first and always,   39
is the confusion of the self,
born of sleep, sloth, and negligence,
is said to be dark happiness.

'No being, whether here on earth,   40
or among the gods in heaven,
is freed from these three qualities,
born of material nature.

'The actions of priests, warriors,   41
commoners and serfs, Arjuna,
are bestowed by the qualities,
which arise from their own natures.

'Calm self-control, uprightness, wisdom,   42
asceticism, purity,
faith and discernment are innate
attributes of the Brahmin class.

'Valor, majesty, firmness, skill,   43
bravery, generosity,
and lordliness are attributes
innate to the warrior class.

'Plowing, trade, and cattle-herding   44
are innate to the commoners;
service to others, the innate
attribute of the class of serfs.

'So a man obtains perfection,   45
pleased by acting from his nature;
hear how, by acting from one's nature,
perfection is achieved by man!

'By worshipping with one's own actions,   46
the Origin of all Beings
by whom the cosmos is pervaded,
perfection is achieved by man.

'Better one's own duty ill-done,   47
than someone else's, well performed;
no one is faulted for performing
acts ordained by one's own nature.

'One should not abandon innate   48
action even though imperfect:
all beginnings are enveloped
by error as fire by smoke.

'Whose intellect is unattached,   49
with self controlled and longings gone,
by renunciation comes to
perfect freedom from all action.

'Now briefly learn from me, Arjuna,   50
how one perfected also then
attains the absolute, which is
the highest state of all knowledge.

'Once yoked with pure intelligence   51
and the self controlled with firmness,
free from sound and all sense-objects,
having put off hate and passion,

'solitary, lightly eating,   52
controlled in body, speech and mind,
meditating, doing yoga,
finding refuge in dispassion,

'having freed oneself from ego,   53
force, pride, anger, lust and grasping,
serene and without selfishness,
one is fit for the absolute.

'One with Brahman, self-untroubled,   54
neither laments nor desires;
impartial among all beings,
he attains perfect love for me.

'He comes to know, by devotion,   55
how great, and who I am, in truth,
then, having known me as I am,
immediately enters me.

'Though he always performs actions,   56
his refuge is in my being;
and by my grace that one attains
the abode which is unchanging.

'Devoted to me as supreme,   57
placing all actions upon me,
your refuge, the yoga of mind,
perpetually think of me!

'Focused on me, due to my grace   58
you will transcend all obstacles;
but if, because of ego, you
do not listen, you will perish.

'If, because of egotism,   59
you think, "No! I will not fight!"
vain is your resolution, for
your own nature will compel you.

'Bound by actions born of your   60
own nature, O Son of Kunti,
you will not act from delusion,
although you act against your will.

'The Lord of All Beings abides   61
in every heart, O Son of Kunti,
spinning all by his magic spells,
as though they were on a turntable.

'Go seek refuge in him only,   62
with your whole being, Arjuna!
By his grace, you will attain that
supreme abode, eternal peace.

'I have declared to you the most   63
secret knowledge in all the world.
Reflect upon all parts of it,
and then do as you wish to do!

'Hear from me now, the supreme word,   64
the greatest secret of them all:
you are indeed my beloved,
so I will speak for your well-being.

'Be mindful of me and devoted,   65
make sacrifices and revere me,
and you will surely go to me
as I promise, for you are dear.

'Relinquishing all your duties,   66
vow to take refuge just in me!
I will cause you to be released
From every evil; do not grieve.

'This should not be spoken ever   67
to one negligent in worship,
nor to one who will not hear it,
nor any who speaks ill of me.

'But he who teaches this supreme   68
secret among my devotees,
giving me perfect devotion,
will go to me without a doubt.

'There will not be another man   69
who gives me greater joy than he,
nor will there be a man dearer
on earth to me than that one is.

'And I would have him worship me   70
by the sacrifice of knowledge,
the one who studies to recite
this sacred discourse of ours.

'And even he who listens to it   71
in good faith and without sneering,
once liberated, may attain
pure worlds of those whose deeds are pure.

'Have you heard this, Son of Pritha,   72
with single-minded concentration?
O Conqueror of Wealth, have you
shed ignorance and confusion?'

"Arjuna said,

'Delusion lost and wisdom gained   73
by your grace, O Unchanging One;
I stand here with all doubt dispelled,
and I will do as you command!'

Sanjaya spoke,

"Thus I have heard this marvelous   74
dialogue between the great-souled
Son of Pritha and Lord Krishna,
which has made my hair stand on end!

"Thanks to Vyasa, I have heard   75
this supreme and secret practice
declared directly by Himself,
Krishna, who is Lord of Yoga.

"O King, repeatedly recalling   76
this marvelous discourse between
Krishna and Arjuna to mind,
I rejoice again and again!

"And repeatedly recalling   77
the marvelous form of Krishna,
great, O King, is my amazement;
again and again, I rejoice!

"Where Krishna, Lord of Yoga, is,   78
where Arjuna the Archer is,
will be splendor, victory, wealth,
and righteousness. So I maintain."

HERE ENDS THE *Bhagavad Gita Upanishad*

NOTES

Introduction

PAGE XXIX. *"On the day"*: from "The Explosion," by Philip Larkin, in *Collected Poems* (New York: Farrar, Straus and Giroux, 2004), p. 154.

Chapter 1

Dhritarashtra said: The blind king sets the *Gita* in motion by asking his minister Sanjaya to describe the battlefield action.

STANZA 1. *the field of Kuru*: Kuru was the mythical ancestor of both the Pandavas and the Kauravas.

the sons of Pandu: The five sons of Pandu are (in age order) Yudhishthira, Bhima, Arjuna, and the twins, Nakula and Sahadeva.

STANZA 2. *King Duryodhana*: The eldest of the Kauravas.

his teacher: Drona, a great warrior and martial arts instructor to both the Kauravas and the Pandavas.

STANZA 3. *the son of Drupada*: Dhrishtadyumna, the twin brother of Draupadi, who is the shared wife of the five sons of Pandu.

STANZA 4. *Bhima*: The Son of Pritha (who was later known as Kunti) by the wind god, Vayu. The strongest of the Pandavas.

Arjuna: Kunti's son by the god Indra and the protagonist of the *Gita*. Arjuna is called "Son of Pritha" or "Son of Kunti" throughout the *Gita*.

Yuyudhana and Virata: Two Pandava warriors. Virata was the king of Matsya, where the disguised Pandavas found refuge in the thirteenth year of their exile.

STANZA 5. *Dhrishtaketu, Chekitana*: Two more Pandava warriors. Their names mean "Daring Brightness" and "Intelligent."

noble king of Kashis: An ally of the Pandavas.

Purujit: Another Pandava warrior, whose name means "Conquering Many."

Kuntibhoga: Prince of the Yadavas, and the foster father of Kunti, mother of the first three Pandavas.

Shaibya: King of the Shibis, an ally of the Pandavas.

STANZA 6. *Yudhamanyu*: Another ally of the Pandavas, whose name means "Passion for Battle."

Uttamauja: Ally of the Pandavas, whose name means "Of Excellent Valor."

Subhadra's son: Abhimanyu was the son of Subhadra, sister of Krishna, and Arjuna's second wife.

Draupadi's sons: Five in number, one by each of the Pandavas. Yudishthira's son was Prativindhya, Bhima's was Sutasoma, Arjuna's was Srutakirti, Satanika was Nakula's, and Srutakarman was Sahadeva's.

STANZA 7. *who are twice-born*: The *Gita* represents the class system that existed in Vedic society. There were four classes: the Brahmans (priests); the nobles or warriors; the commoners; and the serfs. The first three were called "twice-born" because boys of these classes underwent a ritual investiture during which they were given a sacred thread that was worn over the left shoulder.

STANZA 8. *Bhishma*: Though a grand-uncle of the Pandavas, he is fighting against them, reluctantly.

Karna: An unacknowledged half brother of the Pandavas, the first son of Kunti by the sun god, Surya. He is fighting for the Kauravas.

Kripa: Warrior and martial arts instructor of the Kauravas.

Ashvatthaman and Vikarna: Warriors of the Kauravas. Their names mean "Strength of a Horse" and "Large Ears," respectively.

Somadatta's son: A Kauravan warrior prince, whose name means "Gift of Soma." Soma is the name for a Vedic deity and also for an intoxicating drink originally used in sacrifice.

STANZA 14. *Krishna*: When the *Gita* begins, Krishna is a man, a prince of the Yadava clan, who has offered his army to whichever side wants it and his own presence to the opposing side. Duryodhana, the eldest of the Kauravas, chooses

Krishna's army, and Arjuna takes Krishna for the Pandavas, even though he says that he will not fight. Krishna serves, however, as Arjuna's charioteer, and in the course of the *Gita* reveals himself as God incarnate. This revelation culminates in the theophany of chapter 11.

STANZA 17. *Shikandi*: A Pandava warrior born as a girl who was miraculously changed into a man. His name means "Wearing a Tuft of Hair."

Satyaki: Yuyudhana, a Pandava ally, whose name means "Truthful."

STANZA 18. *fierce son of Subhadra*: Subhadra was the daughter of Krishna and wife of Arjuna. Their son was named Abhimanyu.

Drupada: Father of Draupadi, the shared wife of the five Pandavas.

STANZA 20. *Monkey-Bannered Arjuna*: Arjuna's standard was a banner depicting Hanuman, the monkey god who aids Rama in the *Ramayana*.

STANZA 21. *Lord of the Earth, Unshaken One*: Epithets for Krishna.

STANZA 23. *Dhritarashtra's evil son*: His eldest, Duryodhana.

STANZA 24. *O Bharata*: Sanjaya here is addressing King Dhritarashtra, though Krishna uses this epithet for Arjuna.

STANZA 31. *O Handsome-Haired One*: Arjuna's epithet for Krishna.

STANZA 35. *the three worlds*: In Vedic literature the three worlds are the three realms where different gods live: earth, atmosphere, and sky. It is a phrase that simply denotes the entire universe, although some modern uses take it to mean three levels of the universe: physical, subtle, and supreme.

STANZA 37. *O Madhava*: Krishna was a descendant of Madhu, progenitor of the Yadava clan.

STANZA 42. *their ancestors fall . . . water offerings*: War in this world has its consequences in the afterlife for the ancestors. Rice balls and water were common offerings to the dead.

STANZA 44. *damned to dwell eternally / in hell*: Although the text does say "eternally in hell" (*narake niyatam*), a soul's sojourn in hell, or indeed heaven, was not thought to be permanent. As soon as the fruits of bad or good deeds have been reaped, the soul is reborn again.

Chapter 2

STANZA 1. *Madhu-Slaying Krishna*: This epithet comes from an incident in which Krishna slew the demon named Madhu.

STANZA 5. *Tristubh* meter begins in this stanza and continues through stanza 8.

STANZA 9. *the Divine Cowherd*: Another epithet for Krishna, who tended cattle as a youth.

STANZA 22. A single stanza in the *tristubh* meter.

STANZA 31. *your duty as a warrior*: Arjuna cannot consider only his own feelings, since his identity and his destiny have been shaped by his membership in the warrior class.

STANZA 39. *Theory*: The term used here is *Samkhya*, literally, "enumeration" (of the categories, or *tattvas*, that make up the universe). Samkhya was a early system of philosophy which claimed that there are two fundamental kinds of substance: *purusha*, or spirit; and *prakriti*, or matter/nature. The universe that we experience is an unfolding or evolution of *prakriti*, which includes what we regard as mental constituents as well, such as the ego, the intellect, and the mental faculty that perceives thoughts, along with the senses and their objects. The aim of life is to achieve liberation, which is the realization that the individual Self or *purusha* is distinct and isolated from matter. To free the spirit we must discriminate what the spirit is from what it is not (i.e., matter).

Although the *Gita* probably does not specifically mean the school of philosophy in its developed form, Samkhya is central to the *Gita's* vision and its influence can be particularly seen in chapters 13 and 14. Whereas the Samkhya school of philosophy was atheistic, the *Gita*, of course, is theistic.

higher mind: This translates *buddhi*, which can also be rendered as "intellect" or "discrimination." It refers to the first evolute from *prakriti* and reflects the true Self (*purusha*).

in practice now: Although the term *Yoga* is used to denote a distinct system of philosophy, traditionally yoga is the method to realize the truth of Samkhya. In the *Gita* the term has more general application and can be rendered as "practice."

STANZA 42. *The undiscerning . . . in the Vedic ritual*: Krishna here seems to be denigrating the performers of Vedic ritual. This reflects the general rejection of traditional, brahmanical tradition in favor of devotion to a personal God. It also reflects the rise of the warrior class with their own religious traditions against the traditional priests.

STANZA 45. *the three qualities*: These are the three *gunas*, or principles, within *prakriti* that order and control the lower evolutes (*tattva*) from *prakriti*. They are *sattva*, *rajas*, and *tamas*, which can be translated as "lightness" or "purity," "passion," and "darkness" or "inertia." The *gunas* are a very important classification in Hinduism generally, especially for types of food.

the opposing pairs: That is, the pairs of heat and cold, pain and pleasure, light and dark, and so on.

STANZA 55. *his self rests within the Self*: The Sanskrit word *atman* has two designations: one where it is simply a reflexive noun used in the singular to refer to myself, oneself, yourself, or ourselves, and so on; the second where it refers to the eternal self or soul. In one view, this *atman* is identical with Brahman, the ground of all being; in another view, it refers to one's own personal, mortal self. In this translation we have used the uppercase "Self" to indicate the former and the lowercase "self" for the latter.

STANZA 70. A single stanza in the *tristubh* meter.

Chapter 3

STANZA 5. *the nature-born qualities*: That is, the qualities, or *gunas*, born from *prakriti*.

STANZA 10. *Prajapati*: A creator god, whose name means "Lord or Father of Creatures."

your wish-fulfilling cow: In the *Mahabharata*, Surabhi is the "cow of wishes," a sacred cow who granted human wishes and desires.

STANZA 15. *Brahman*: The term Brahman denotes the impersonal, absolute reality. Originally it meant the power of the sacrifice but then came to mean the power that pervades the entire cosmos. The *Gita* (8.20–22) tells us that the Supreme Person, the personal God Krishna, is a higher truth than the impersonal, imperishable absolute. Those who reach Brahman are liberated, but God, the Supreme Person, is attained only by those with devotion (*bhakti*).

STANZA 20. *Janaka*: Legendary warrior-king, one of the great sages.

Chapter 4

STANZA 1. *Vivasvat*: The Hindu god of the sun, father of Manu.

Manu: A giver of laws and the progenitor of the human race.

Ikshvaku: Manu's son and the founder of a dynasty of kings.

Chapter 5

STANZA 4. *Fools say, "Theory and practice / are different!"*: Samkhya and Yoga were closely related traditions. Samkhya was regarded as the theoretical or metaphysical backdrop to Yoga. Yoga assumed the Samkhya categories (*tattva*) and general theory of the development of the cosmos and person. Similarly, Samkhya was thought to be not simply a philosophy but an intellectual practice that brought a person to spiritual liberation.

STANZA 13. *the city of nine gates*: The human body, with its nine orifices considered as "gates."

STANZA 18. *a dog-cooking outcaste*: One of the lowest of the low, technically outside of the class system (that is, *avarna* rather than *varna*).

STANZA 24. *extinction*: Extinction (*nirvana*) is a Buddhist term that the *Gita* here uses to signify the ultimate state of liberation in Brahman.

Chapter 6

STANZA 44. *the Word-Brahman*: At one level, the Word-Brahman (*shabda-brahman*) is the Veda as revealed sound or word. At another, it is the absolute reality in the form of sound that becomes manifest in thought and speech.

Chapter 7

STANZA 4. *my material nature*: Here Krishna is referring to the manifestations or evolutes of matter (*prakriti*); in due order, the higher mind or intellect (*buddhi*); the ego (*ahamkara*); the mind (*manas*); and the five elements.

STANZA 5. *my other, / higher nature*: Here Krishna refers to the evolutes of nature or matter (*prakriti*) being of two kinds, the lower referring to the evolutes themselves, the higher to the souls who are bound within nature.

STANZA 8. *the* Vedas' *sacred syllable*: That is, the syllable OM. This sound or mantra is regarded as the essence of the universe, the sonic form of God.

STANZA 12. *states of being*: The different kinds of beings in the universe, and the various kinds of deity, humans, animals, and plants, are all governed by the three material natures, or *gunas*: lightness or purity; passion; and darkness or inertia.

STANZA 25. *Hidden by my magic power*: Magic power (*maya*) can also mean "illusion" and is a term identified with ignorance in the Vedanta school of philosophy.

Chapter 8

STANZA 8. *the Supreme Person*: That is, Krishna. Here God is conceived not as an impersonal absolute power (Brahman) but as a personal deity.

STANZA 9. The beginning of three stanzas in the *tristubh* meter.

One meditating on the ancient poet: "The poet (*kavi*)" seems to be a reference to the Supreme Person, although in the *Vedas* "the poet" can be an epithet of Agni, the god of fire.

STANZA 17. *a Brahmanic day*: Chapter 9, stanzas 7 and 8,

expands on the nature of the *Kalpa*, a period of 4.3 billion years, at the end of which, the world is annihilated.

STANZA 23. *where . . . / those departed yogis go*: This refers to the doctrine of the afterlife found in the *Brihadaranyaka Upanishad* (6.2:15–16) and the *Chandogya Upanishad* (5.10: 1–2). Those texts say that at death the deceased travels by either two paths, one path leading to the gods and ending in Brahman, from which there is no return to this world, the other ending in the moon and followed by reincarnation in this world. The *Gita* (8.24–26) refers to these as the northern and southern paths.

STANZA 28. Chapter 8 concludes with a stanza in the *tristubh* meter.

Chapter 9

STANZA 16. *ghee*: Clarified butter.

STANZA 17. *soma-strainer*: A device for straining fruits. In Vedic sacrifice, it was used for straining the juices of the soma plant. Soma was a vision-producing substance of vegetable origin employed in Vedic sacrifices. Its source is unknown, though it has been identified with the stimulant ephedra by some and by others with *Amanita muscaria*, a psychedelic mushroom.

the three chief Vedas: The *Rig*, *Sama*, and *Yajur Vedas*.

STANZA 20. The next two stanzas are in the *tristubh* meter.

longed-for world of Indra: Indra is the main Vedic deity, a great warrior and drinker of soma.

STANZA 32. *out of evil wombs*: Rebirths regarded as bad because traditionally thought to exclude the possibility of liberation.

Chapter 10

STANZA 6. *the seven great seers*: Kashyapa, Atri, Vashishta, Vishvamitra, Gotama, Jamadagni, and Bhadradvaja. They are identified with the stars of Ursa minor.

the four law-giving Manus: At the beginning of each of the four ages (*yuga*) a Manu appears who gives the law.

STANZA 13. *the divine seer Narada*: A sage, the composer of some Vedic hymns.

Asita, Devala . . . Vyasa: The names of legendary sages. Vyasa was the legendary author of the *Mahabharata* (and so also the *Bhagavad Gita*).

STANZA 17. *Yogin*: The consonant stem of the word. In the nominative singular, it is yogī, which we have rendered as "yogi," in accordance with common practice.

STANZA 19. *my own / divine self-manifestations*: These are the forms in which God or Krishna appears in the world.

STANZA 21. *Of the Adityas . . . Vishnu*: The Adityas are celestial gods in the *Veda*.

of storm gods . . . Marici: Marici is the chief of the storm gods or Maruts.

STANZA 22. *Of* Vedas, *the* Sama Veda: The *Sama* is one of the collections (*samhita*) of hymns (much of which reproduces the *Rig Veda*) that contain instructions on chanting the verses. The text was recited during Vedic sacrifice.

of the gods . . . Vasava: Another name for Indra, the most important Vedic deity.

STANZA 23. *Of the Rudras . . . Shiva*: The Rudras are storm gods. Rudra is an early name for Shiva, who became one of the main three gods of medieval Hinduism along with Vishnu and the Goddess (Devi). In the mythology of Vishnu he is regarded as the destroyer of the universe, with Brahma as the creator and Vishnu as the preserver or maintainer.

of Rakshasas, Kubera: The Rakshasas are a group of demons and Kubera is their leader, the Lord of Wealth associated with the north.

I am Agni: The fire god or flame itself.

I am Meru: Meru is a mythical mountain residing at the center of the universe and supporting the heavens. The gods dwell there.

STANZA 24. *the chief of household priests*: The chief priest, or *hotri*, would recite verses from the *Rig Veda* during Vedic sacrifice.

Skanda: Skanda is the god of war and son of Shiva. He is the chief general who leads the army of the gods against the demons.

STANZA 25. *Bhrigu*: An ancient sage in the *Rig Veda*.

STANZA 26. *the sacred fig*: The fig tree is sacred in Hinduism. It is a symbol of the entire cosmos (as we will see in chapter 15, stanza 1).

Narada: A famous sage who appears frequently in religious literature.

of Gandharvas, Citraratha: Citraratha ("He whose chariot is Bright") is the king of the Gandharvas or heavenly musicians.

Kapila: An ancient sage said to be the founder of the Samkhya school of philosophy.

STANZA 27. *the one Indra rides*: Indra's horse came out of the nectar that was produced in the mythical churning of the ocean.

of elephants, / Indra's lordly Airavata: The elephant that Indra rides.

STANZA 28. *Kandarpa, god of love*: Also called Kama, Desire.

Vasuki: The king of snakes.

STANZA 29. *Of Naga-snakes . . . Ananta*: The Nagas are supernatural snake-beings whose king is Ananta. Ananta is also depicted in mythology as the snake whose coils encircle the earth and on whom Vishnu sleeps.

of water-creatures . . . Varuna: Varuna is an ancient Vedic water god, king of aquatic animals.

Aryaman: The king of the ancestors.

Yama: The god of death.

STANZA 30. *Prahlada*: The king of the demons or Daityas, who became a devotee of Vishnu.

Vainateya: Garuda, the son of Vinata, the great bird on whom Vishnu rides.

STANZA 31. *Rama*: The warrior who is the hero of the *Ramayana*.

Makara of the sea monsters: The greatest of sea monsters.

STANZA 34. *I am death, the all-destroying*: This is the verse quoted by J. Robert Oppenheimer upon seeing the first

successful detonation of an atomic bomb: "Now I am
become Death, the destroyer of worlds."

STANZA 35. *Of Saman-chants, Bhradsama*: A type of Vedic
meter in chanting the verses.

of meters . . . Gayatri: A type of meter in the *Rig Veda*.

STANZA 36. *I am the gambling of cheats*: There is nowhere
where Krishna is not, even in gambling.

STANZA 37. *Of the Vrishnis . . . Krishna*: The Vrishnis are a clan
from whom Krishna is descended.

Vyasa: The legendary author of the *Mahabharata*.

Ushana: An ancient sage.

Chapter 11

STANZA 3. *I desire to behold your / lordly form*: Here Arjuna asks
to see Krishna's universal, majestic, or lordly form (*aish-
varam rupam*) in contrast to his human form.

STANZA 6. *the Adityas and Vasus, / the Rudras, Ashvins and
Maruts*: These are all different kinds of deity in the *Veda*.
The Adityas are celestial deities; the Vasus are gods of the
atmosphere ruled by Indra; the Rudras are storm gods
associated with Rudra or Shiva; the Ashvins are divine
twins who are physicians; and the Maruts are storm gods
sometimes identified with the Rudras.

STANZA 9. *Vishnu*: This is one of the three references to
Vishnu in the *Gita*. The later religion of Vishnu identified
Krishna as an incarnation (*avatara*) of Vishnu, but the *Gita*
itself clearly presents Krishna as the supreme deity. In a

sense Krishna is an incarnation of himself along with other manifestations or *vibhutis* (listed in chapter 10). The term *avatara* is not used in the text.

STANZA 15. An extended passage in the *tristubh* meter commences here and continues until stanza 50.

STANZA 17. *armed with mace and discus*: In plastic representations these are held by Krishna and/or Vishnu in his two-armed form.

STANZA 22. *Rudras . . . the Perfected*: A list of gods, ancestors, sages, and those who have attained perfection.

STANZA 33. *O Ambidextrous Archer*: Arjuna is a skilled bowman.

STANZA 34. *Jayadratha, Karna*: These are Kauravas, enemies of Arjuna but also belonging to his family.

STANZA 39. *Vayu, Yama, Varuna*: Respectively, the god of winds, the god of death, and the god of water.

the Great-Grandfather: The primal ancestor.

STANZA 41. *Yadava*: The name of the clan that Krishna belonged to.

STANZA 51. As Krishna resumes his mortal form, the poet returns to the *shloka* meter, which continues to the end of this chapter.

Chapter 13

O Handsome-Haired One: Chapter 13 begins with an unnumbered stanza, the only one in the *Gita*. If it were counted, the poem would number 701 stanzas rather than 700.

of the field and of its knower: This chapter is an important discourse about the nature of the self. The field is life, the experience of the world, though the senses and the knower of the field is the self within the body that undergoes experience in the world through the senses.

STANZA 5. *The great elements . . . sense-action*: This is a list of the Samkhya evolutes or *tattvas* from matter (*prakriti*).

STANZA 12. *the birthless, matchless Brahman, said / neither to be nor to be not*: The object of knowledge here is Brahman, the absolute, which is beyond the duality of being and not-being, existence and non-existence. This is paradoxical in that Brahman cannot really be an object of knowledge in any conventional sense although the realization of Brahman is a liberating cognition.

STANZA 13. *Its hand and foot . . . its eye, head, face*: The entire universe is the body of God.

STANZA 21. *good and bad wombs*: Cf. the note at chapter 9, stanza 32.

STANZA 22. *The highest spirit*: Here the "spirit" (*purusha*) refers to the Self within the body, which is individual to some extent and distinct from God, although supported and sustained by God.

STANZA 24. *Samkhya yoga*: On the discipline of Samkhya, see the note at chapter 2, stanza 39.

Chapter 14

STANZA 1. *the highest knowledge*: That is, knowledge of Krishna as the absolute.

STANZA 5. *Purity, passion and darkness*: The three qualities or *gunas*.

Chapter 15

STANZA 1. *an eternal fig tree*: Literally, the tree "under which horses stand." The fig tree is a symbol of the entire cosmos. Here the image of the tree is inverted, with its roots in heaven and its branches on earth, the nourishment of the world in the form of the *Vedas* coming from a higher world.

STANZA 2. Stanzas 2–5 are composed in the *tristubh* meter.

STANZA 4. *And I take refuge*: Krishna here is speaking from the perspective of a devotee.

STANZA 5. *that changeless realm*: The true abode, the abode of Krishna.

STANZA 8. *When the Lord*: Here the text refers to God incarnating in the world, but the idea that the Self takes certain attributes with it when it leaves this body for the next is pertinent to all beings.

STANZA 13. *juicy soma, Lord of Plants*: See the note at chapter 9, stanza 17.

STANZA 14. *digestive fire*: Digestion was considered to be a form of fire.

STANZA 15. A single stanza in the *tristubh* meter.

Vedanta: The end of the *Veda*, referring to the *Upanishads* and also to the system of philosophy grounded in the interpretation of the *Vedas* and *Upanishads*.

Chapter 16

STANZA 23. *The commands / of scripture*: The *Vedas*.

Chapter 17

STANZA 5. *Who suffer dread austerities*: Krishna cautions against extreme asceticism, which does not free one from attachment.

STANZA 7. *Each of the three kinds*: That is, the three qualities (*guna*) of purity, passion, and darkness.

STANZA 23. *"OM THAT [IS] TRUTH"*: This is a Sanskrit mantra that is thought to contain the essence of Brahman.

Chapter 18

BEFORE STANZA 74. *Sanjaya spoke*: We return to complete the frame of the *Bhagavad Gita*, with a reminder that the entire work is the reportage of Sanjaya to the blind king, Dhritarashtra.

5/12-1 (6/... ..)
8/12-2
4/19-8

OYSTER BAY – E NORWICH PUB LIBY
89 EAST MAIN ST
OYSTER BAY, NY 11771
(516) 922 – 1212

BAKER & TAYLOR

APR 1 0 2012